PRIVATE INVESTIGATION STRATEGIES AND TECHNIQUES
The World's Greatest Private Eye Reveals Her Secrets

PRIVATE INVESTIGATION STRATEGIES AND TECHNIQUES

The World's Greatest Private Eye Reveals Her Secrets

by Angela Woodhull

Loompanics Unlimited
Port Townsend, Washington

Private Investigation Strategies and Techniques
The World's Greatest Private Eye Reveals Her Secrets
© 2001 by Angela Woodhull

Published by:
Loompanics Unlimited
PO Box 1197
Port Townsend, WA 98368
Loompanics Unlimited is a division of Loompanics Enterprises, Inc.
Phone: 360-385-2230
E-mail: service@loompanics.com
Web site: www.loompanics.com

Cover art by Harlan Kramer

ISBN 1-55950-214-2
Library of Congress Card Catalog Number 2001086814

Contents

Dedication

This book is dedicated to my three grandchildren, Tyler, Cody, and Alexandria. I hope that at least one of them will grow up and appreciate their weird ass grandmother.

Introduction

This is a book about real cases investigated by a real P.I. You'll find the stories contained in this book to be entertaining, sometimes hilarious, as well as informative. I consider myself creative at what I do, which is one of the most important ingredients for success in this business. With a little ingenuity, anyone can learn to use the tools that are suggested in this book.

Some tools to get you started:

1. **A good database.** I prefer to use DBT (Data Base Technologies), located in Ft. Lauderdale, Florida. DBT reports contain the name, Social Security number, driver's license number, address (current and former) for the subject and his or her relatives, neighbors, spouses, property, vehicles, professional licenses, and criminal history. Sometimes the information may be a little outdated, or even inaccurate, but there is usually something on the report to help me get started. Sometimes, DBT is all I need to complete an investigation. For instance, a while back, a 41-year-old woman contacted me and said she had been

adopted at birth. She wanted to find her blood mother who was 16 at the time of her birth. Luckily, she did have a name for the blood mother, but being it was 41 years ago, I doubted we would find her under that name. However, checking DBT, we used the maiden name as a middle name. Voila! A hit! Within a few minutes, I was able to locate a birth mom and put her daughter in touch with her.

2. **Courthouse records. Rap sheets.** Sometimes, you'll want to do a **thorough** investigation on someone. For instance, executive profiling is a big business right now. This means that you would start off by generating a DBT report, but then you would follow-up by going in person to each and every county where the person has lived and double-checking the courthouse records and the rap sheets at the local sheriff departments and police departments. If you are not being paid for your travel, you would contact a fellow or sister P.I. and subcontract with them to check the records for you.

Good luck in your quest to become an expert private eye. And I hope you have as much fun as I have in solving the wide variety of mysteries that will come your way.

Chapter One
Recipe for Success

What makes a person successful as a P.I.? If I had to write a "recipe for success," here would be the main ingredients:

1. **Listening skills.** The ability to listen carefully and empathically to a client is very important. Recently, I was contacted by a man who had had an affair with an old girlfriend who was now married. He was under the impression, when she recontacted him after seven years, that she still loved him and desired to leave her husband if their secret affair proved to develop into a positive, working relationship. But after investing three and a half years of time, money, and emotions, the man concluded that she was never going to leave her husband. In fact, she confessed to him that her husband knew all along about their affair.

   The man concluded that he was being used, being made a fool, by the woman and her husband. At first, when he contacted me, he wanted me to "gain evidence," so he could sue her for using him and for "intentional infliction of emotional distress." We talked at great length during our first meeting. I told him my impression was that the woman was not being intentionally malevolent, but merely thoughtless and self-centered. During subsequent phone conversations, my client came to accept this perspective. In all, he paid me $350 simply for listening to him. We never did investigate his ex-lover.

2. **Professionalism.** A physician hired me to interview the boyfriend of one of his former employees who was fired. Shortly after the woman was terminated, the doctor received a call, allegedly from the IRS, claiming that he was about to be investigated. He hired me to go speak directly with the boyfriend, get his side of the story, and warn him that if he did, in fact, place the call, he could be arrested for impersonating a government agent. Also, the former employee had allegedly extorted about $6,000 in funds from the doctor's office. By talking directly and professionally with the boyfriend, I was able to get the matter resolved, and have the funds returned, without the doctor having to press charges against the boyfriend.

3. **An excellent memory.** An attorney hired me to speak with a landlady who was pressing criminal charges against her former tenant for stealing and forging a check. I listened carefully and was able to write up a full report regarding what the landlady would claim in court. The attorney won the case; the criminal charges against her client were dropped.

4. **Poly-directional thinking.** An attorney sent me to a small town to find witnesses regarding his client who hit a cow with her car. No one wanted to come forward and speak. The one woman whose name appeared on the police report as a potential witness could not be located. She listed only a P.O. box and no phone number. By go-

ing directly to city hall and posing as one of the woman's friends, I was able to obtain her home address and phone number and also her place of employment.

5. **The ability to create pretexts.** Private investigators need to be able to create a wide variety of believable characters to get a job done. My pretexts (covers/disguises) have included pretending I am a journalist, cleaning lady, real estate investor, welfare mother, and prostitute, to name a few. Creating pretexts has been easy for me since I have played such a wide variety of roles in real life. During my 50 years, I have had many jobs and I have interacted with a wide variety of people. I have worked as a college professor, a waitress, a dry cleaning presser, a door-to-door salesperson, a schoolteacher, mentor, bookkeeper, seminar leader, singing telegram delivery person, musician, author, journalist, surveyor, sales clerk, and housecleaner. I also grew up in an amusement park. My father owned food concessions and a basketball stand at a summer carnival and at a baseball field, so I have had lots of contact with the public from a very early age.

6. **Being honest.** Despite the many pretexts that I use to obtain the information that my clients seek, I am basically a very honest, straightforward person. My clients realize this and they trust me implicitly. Because of my honest nature, I do not come across as an undercover agent. When people discover that I am a private investigator they are generally, at first, shocked and disbelieving.

7. **Salesmanship skills.** When potential clients contact my business, I have about one minute to convince them that I am the best. Telling them I'm a Ph.D. and an educational psychologist generally helps clinch the sale, but so does

explaining to them that I will work carefully and closely with them.

8. **ESP.** A lot of what I do is based on hunch. You might call this ESP, or extra sensory perception. How do you know whether or not you have ESP? Trying running an experiment on yourself. Here's what I did recently with my partner, D.H. We were having lunch at Quincy's Steak House. Oftentimes, when I'm eating out I will engage the waitperson in a conversation. I told her, "Okay. Ask me about anybody in here, and I'll tell you three things about them." She pointed to the young man who was running the cash register. I said, "Okay, he's currently enrolled in college. He likes to work out at the gym. His girlfriend recently dumped him because she thought he was too boring." (The last one I threw in just to be funny).

She looked at me in amazement. "You are absolutely right," she said, "on all three counts. I know. Because I am his ex-girlfriend." Soon, the entire waitstaff was approaching me. "Do me! Do me! That other waitress says that you're psychic."

I told one woman, "You are very angry at your mother right now." (Truthfully, I really can't explain to you why I said this. It was just a hunch based upon that "voice" I sometimes hear in my head.) Her eyes grew very wide. "How did you **know** that?" she exclaimed. I replied, "I can just tell." She confessed, "My mother gave my new, private, unlisted telephone number to my ex-boyfriend."

"Okay. Here's what you do," I told her. "Your ex-boyfriend will call you, but only one time. Be polite to him and tell him you are not interested in resuming any romantic relationship with him. He won't call you again. Then, call your mother, and instead of spazzing out on her, like you usually do, just tell her in a calm manner what you did when your ex-boyfriend called, and tell her you would appreciate her not divulging your personal phone number to anyone ever again. Because you will remain calm, your mother will react differently toward you."

"How did you know all that? How did you know that I spazz out on my mother?"

"I don't know," I replied. "It was just a hunch."

Test your own ESP. Have friends provide you with photos of loved ones and friends. See how much you can "read" about these people whom you have never met. If you have a high number of hits, this is a sign that you have a talent, which is very useful to private investigation.

9. **The ability to write clearly and with detail.** When I compose a report for a client, I do not spare them any details. By adding everything to the report that I can possibly remember, the client feels that I have done a thorough job. Also, most clients enjoy reading all the details. In fact, the more juicy the details, the more your clients will love you.

10. **Keen observationist.** Are you good at observing your surroundings and paying close attention to detail? One night, I was eating supper at a Chinese restaurant with my husband and a friend. Suddenly, I noticed an Asian man disconnecting one of the keyboards that sat on the small stage where live weekend entertainment is performed by a one-man band. At first, noticing that he was of Asian descent, I assumed he was an employee or relative of the owner. But after unhooking the keyboard, I noticed that he simply tucked it under his arm and exited the restaurant. Something was not right. Most musicians

carry their instruments in cases to protect them. I sprang up from the table and told the owner what I just witnessed.

Indeed, the man was a thief, he said. A report was taken, and I provided the police with a detailed description of the man. The owner knew the man's friends, who frequently patronize the restaurant, and, hence, he was able to get back his $1,700 keyboard and press criminal charges. At the time when the man stole the keyboard, the restaurant was packed with several customers. Amazingly, no one even noticed what the man was doing. However, while carrying on a conversation with my husband and our friend, I was also observing everything and everyone in the restaurant. It is amazing that out of about 50 people, I was the only one who took notice of the thief.

Chapter Two
How to Sell Your Services

In the beginning, most of your business will be generated from the Yellow Pages. The majority of your callers will start off with the same, identical question: "How much would it cost if I hired you to do thus and so?"

The best way to handle this question, I've discovered, is to inform them, "Well, I'm not quite sure if that is the right question. There are many P.I.s who may give you a lower price, but they may not get you any results. In the end, you won't have saved any money if they have been unable to obtain the results you wanted. Now, before I tell you my prices, may I tell you a little bit about myself and how I operate?"

After detailing some of the strategies I use, I then ask them what they would like me to accomplish specifically. I give them a menu of strategies I can use to accomplish the assignment. I let them decide which strategy they would like me to employ. (Prices vary; for instance, surveillance using several P.I.s is obviously much more expensive than if I talk to the subject directly as an undercover cosmetic sales lady.)

I tell them that they will be involved in every aspect of the investigation, and I promise them that I will contact them every time something new develops. In this way, I have managed to keep all of my clients happy. I have never had someone refuse to pay or demand a refund. Also, at the time of this writing, I am still batting 1,000: I have never not obtained the information that a client was seeking.

Chapter Three
Cheaters!

A lot of the callers you'll get from the Yellow Pages will want to know whether or not their spouse is cheating on them. Even in states where there is no-fault divorce, such as Florida, people still want to know the answer to this important question. First of all, to know the truth brings with it a sense of peace. Most people suspect when a spouse is cheating and, at first, will confront the cheater. In most cases, the cheater does not come forth with an admission. Instead, they tell the accuser that they are insane, paranoid, or living in a fantasy world. These kinds of statements only add to the anguish that the cheated-upon spouse may be feeling. Second, there are child custody issues and alimony issues. Oftentimes, judges will, indeed, factor cheating into consideration when they are determining which parent will be the primary custodian and how much alimony an ex-spouse will receive.

These kinds of jobs require a lot of "hand-holding." Expect to spend a lot of time during the initial consultation listening to your clients as they describe the mental anguish that the cheating spouse has been putting them through. In many cases, there will be tears. This is where expert listening skills come in handy. Your client may want you to be more of a friend and a counselor than a P.I. Many P.I.s will not even take on these kinds of cases because they require so much intense and emotional interaction. Some P.I.s are also afraid that a needy client will call too frequently, but I have never found this to be the case. I have discovered that if I listen carefully, thoroughly, and with great empathy during the initial visit, the clients feel that I understand them. They are confident that I am "going to bat" for them. I have literally held hands and cried with my clients during the initial visit.

In this chapter, you'll learn strategies and techniques for discovering whether or not a spouse is cheating. Don't automatically assume that the spouse is, in fact, cheating. As you'll see below, there was no evidence that cheating had taken place in two cases.

José, His Wife Lucy, and His Half-Brother Andrew

José sat with me in a quiet upstairs lobby room at the Holiday Inn. In between bursts of anguish, sobs, and a plethora of tears, he described how he had done everything in life to become a success while, simultaneously, attempting to nurture his extended family. When José was 10 years old, his mother committed suicide. His father had died of a heart attack shortly after abandoning the family when José was eight. At his mother's grave, José vowed that he would help his half-brother, his sister, and his cousin, Lucy, so that they would grow up to be happy and successful people.

In his early twenties, José married his beautiful cousin, Lucy, and they moved to the United States where he began his college education. Two years ago, while working on his

Ph.D. in chemical engineering, José invited his half-brother, Andrew, and his sister, Louisa, to come live with him. Both his sister and his wife decided to attend the college of nursing, while his younger half-brother, Andrew, became seriously interested in weight-lifting and computer programming. Together, José and Lucy produced two beautiful daughters, who were eight and 10 years old at that time when I met José.

José had rented a large, ranch-style home in an upscale section of town. With grant monies from both Brazil and the United States, he was able to support the entire household on his stipends. But something was amiss. About a year before he contacted me, José noticed that Lucy was paying a lot of attention to her cousin and brother-in-law, Andrew. She would go out of her way to prepare him an extra-special breakfast, saying that he needed the additional helping of protein to keep up his stamina at the gym. She would fuss over him, have lunch with him, and always be looking for an excuse to go grocery shopping or take in a movie with him.

José had to go back to Brazil for six weeks to take care of business. When he returned, the situation seemed even worse than it was before. He started making outright accusations. His brother left in a huff and spent the night in a hotel. Lucy also left for a few hours saying she was disgusted that José would even think such a terrible thing! Even José's sister scolded him for lodging such cruel and bizarre accusations.

Going strongly on his hunches, José did not back down. Instead, he purchased a special computer program that would print out and forward to him the e-mail messages that he believed Andrew was secretly sending to Lucy. That's when José discovered that his "hunches" were not so far-fetched after all. It was the day after he printed out the first batch of revealing messages and e-mail love letters that José contacted me.

We sat in the Holiday Inn, holding hands, while José interpreted the secret messages written in Portuguese. One message said that Lucy was the most beautiful woman in the world. Another message laughed and poked fun at José, saying what a sexless, serious fuddy-duddy he was. A third said they were looking forward to meeting at the hotel that evening where Andrew promised to shower the beautiful Lucy with plenty of hugs and kisses.

José took off his glasses to wipe the tears that were streaming down the bridge of his nose. I handed him an additional Kleenex tissue and squeezed his hands tightly.

"What have I done to deserve this?" he sobbed. "I have worked hard to provide nice things for my family. True, I have not been as attentive to my wife as I should be, but I am in the middle of writing a Ph.D. dissertation. It is a very intense and energy-draining process. My brother, on the other hand, is very gifted with engaging in woman-talk. He sits with my sister and my wife for hours listening to their stories, paging through women's magazines with them. He comes downstairs into the kitchen in the morning, wearing only a pair of shorts, his knees dropped open, flexing his muscles. My wife rushes to pour him a cup of coffee. They kept telling me how crazy I am. And now I have this." He held up the printed e-mails and wailed loudly.

José didn't feel that the e-mails would be good enough for court. His goal was to divorce his wife and obtain primary custody of his two daughters. He believed that Lucy and Andrew would claim that he, José, had actually created those e-mails himself in an attempt to gain verification for his paranoid thoughts. Now, he wanted to know what I could do to catch them. He was afraid that time was running out. Andrew had just graduated and obtained a good job as a computer programmer. He had already put a deposit on a fancy condominium in town. As soon as his brother moved into his own place, there would be no way of proving that Lucy and Andrew were having an affair. He tried to make me reassure him time and time again throughout our lengthy initial conversation, that I would, indeed, catch them at a hotel or out in public kissing, and that this evidence would absolutely be a full-proof guarantee that he would obtain full custody of his daughters. Of course, I could not provide him with any kind of guarantee. I assured him that I would do my best.

José wanted to be closely, carefully, and continuously involved in every step of the investigation. This is where I differ with my fellow P.I.s. Most of them would not allow such a thing. I find that I get more accomplished. First of all, my client knows the comings and goings of his mate far better than I do. Second, if I am unable to "catch" the couple, I am left blameless. After all, I simply followed José's directives.

The first step was to observe Lucy when she went to the Health Science Library to study for her upcoming nursing examinations. José was convinced that she was not spending long afternoons at the library. Instead, he believed that Andrew was meeting her there and together they would go off to a hotel for a couple of hours.

We also drove together to several of the area hotels, posing as Lucy and Andrew, claiming that we lost our receipt for our last stay and asking the desk clerk to print out a duplicate. Indeed, we discovered two occasions when Andrew had registered at local hotels. Again, José didn't feel the evidence was great enough to confront them, however. He felt that Andrew would simply claim he slept there alone.

I took along my partner, D.H., for this job. We managed to find friends from the health care profession who fitted me with a pair of green scrubs and him with a physician's lab coat and a stethoscope. D.H. sat just outside the library, reading a book, while I went inside and sat at a nearby table observing Lucy.

On our first visit, Lucy got up several times and went either to the water fountain, the bathroom, or the pay phone where she made furtive calls to her lover, speaking to him in whispered tones in Portuguese. Of course, we had no idea what she was saying. After a while, I started to feel like Mary's little lamb. And Lucy told her husband that there was a strange woman at the library who was following her everywhere.

On our second visit, both D.H. and I stationed ourselves just outside of the library. Lucy had managed to depart the first time and we both missed her. This time we placed ourselves at the north and south exits and agreed that only the one of us in the direction she was headed would follow her out of the building. But, again, Lucy was very clever. As I walked behind her, she stepped up the pace. Soon, she was running. I began running, too, and I didn't care if she saw me. I knew she was fleeing to her lover and I wanted to capture the moment. Lucy was much more familiar with the maze in the medical building than I. We went up and down stairs, in and out of elevators, and around bends until finally she lost me. By the time I caught up with my partner, I was so flustered and out of breath, I felt I could do bodily harm to someone.

They say that "three is a charm," and in this case, that old saying proved to be correct. Andrew had already started moving into his condominium and José had done a good job of finding the paperwork. With his condo apartment number in hand, I went to the office of the complex and told them I was doing an undercover investigation on a drug dealer who was about to move onto the premises. I showed them my license. With that pretext in place, the office did provide me with a secret code for opening the locked security gate that would get me onto the premises.

José called and said, "You'd better come right now. I just got home from the university and Lucy says she wants the car so she can go to the library and study. But I don't think she's on her way to the library. I think she's going straight to Andrew's new condo."

On this occasion, I also took along my husband, I.J., who was driving a mail delivery van. I stationed I.J. at the end of José and Lucy's street heading east, while D.H. was with me, heading west. Sure enough, within minutes of our arriving, Lucy pulled out from her street and turned left (west). Very soon, she noticed in her rear view mirror that she was being followed by us, but she continued along her path, assuming that two bungling P.I.s would not be able to get into the premises of her lover's condo complex. When she saw that we did enter the complex, she simply parked her car at the office, which was quite a distance from building Q, where Andrew was beginning to reside. I quickly dropped off D.H. in the woods with his camera across from building Q, while I.J. circled the perimeter of the complex with his mail truck. I remained parked at the office so that Lucy would think she had foiled us. Little did she know that as she rushed into Andrew's condo, she was being videotaped by D.H. who was hiding in the forest.

An hour passed, and there was no sign of D.H. or of I.J., who continued to circle the complex with his own video camera ready to shoot. I decided to find I.J. and tell him to station himself somewhere outside the back door, so we would have cameras aimed at both of Andrew's exits. Right then, as I drove down the road inside the complex, I saw D.H. coming toward me, Andrew beside him. D.H. had an absolutely terrified expression on his face. As I stopped the van and unlocked the passenger door, Andrew blocked D.H. from entering my van. Instead, he spoke in a loud tone, demanded to know who we were, and attempted to wrestle

D.H. for his video camera. (Apparently, when Lucy was exiting his condo, Andrew saw D.H. in the woods videotaping her.) D.H. fell to the ground when Andrew elbowed him in the ribs. I quickly exited the van and began knocking on residents' doors, all to no avail, calling for the police. Meanwhile, D.H., cradling the video camera to his chest, managed to pick himself off the ground, run to the driver's side, and enter the van. I rushed back into the passenger seat, but Andrew reached into the van, turned off the ignition, and confiscated the keys. Now, a tug of war over the camera strap, which was around D.H.'s arm, ensued. Andrew pulled in his direction and I pulled toward me, leaving large bruises on D.H.'s arm. Finally, I dug my nails into Andrew's wrist, hard enough to draw blood, and he let go of the camera strap. I quickly took the camera from D.H. and hurled it into the back of my van. Right then, an off-duty sheriff pulled up. I exited my vehicle, out of breath, flashed my I.D. and announced that we were P.I.s. Andrew kept interrupting and screaming saying that he, too, wanted to press charges on us for invading his privacy. The sheriff called for on-duty police and ordered the three of us to wait in the office.

While waiting inside the office lobby, I called José and told him what had just transpired. He took a taxi to the complex and joined us for the rest of the transaction. When he arrived, his wife burst into tears and went over to José for protection and comfort. They spoke heatedly in Portuguese and then José said that he did not want us to press any charges against his brother, that it would ruin his family. D.H. and I felt baffled. The sheriffs handled the situation very well. They interviewed each of us separately and then played hardball with Andrew, telling him that they would arrest him for assault and battery and attempting to steal my van. (He admitted he had taken the keys.) They released him and gave us a copy of the incident report.

A few days passed before we heard again from José. That night, using his sister as a witness, he confronted his wife. At first, she continued to deny that any kind of affair had been taking place. She said she was simply going to visit her brother-in-law and help him unpack his possessions. Then, he brought out the e-mails. As he read them aloud, in front of his wife and sister, at first, Lucy admitted that they had sinned on only one occasion. So, he continued to read, and an hour or so into the interrogation, she fully admitted to everything.

José purchased plane tickets for Brazil. I wrote a report regarding what had transpired. In Rio de Janeiro, José did obtain full custody of his children, based in large part on what I stated in the report. When he returned to the United States, we met for lunch and he thanked me profusely. Meanwhile, his half-brother, Andrew, split for California. Lucy begged José not to divorce her. He said he would continue to live with her in the United States, but he was free to date (although he's not doing so). Last time he called me, he and his ex-wife were still living together, and apparently, there is no more contact between the two of them and Andrew. José said that if his wife remains faithful to him for a year, he will forgive her and remarry her.

When the state prosecuting attorney's office contacted us, we dropped all charges against Andrew. Mission accomplished.

Points to Remember: What made this assignment a success?

1. **Sometimes, it actually helps if the subjects know they are being followed.** After a while, they will feel so self-confident that you are just a bumbling P.I. and that you

will never catch them, they will take risky chances. By driving straight to Andrew's condo, Lucy guaranteed that she was going to get busted.

2. **Sometimes, it also pays to videotape the subject in plain view.** D.H. told me afterward that he intentionally allowed Andrew to "catch" him videotaping Lucy's exiting his condo. By starting an altercation, Andrew guaranteed that José would get the information he so desperately desired.

3. **Hand-holding is a crucial skill.** Because I empathized with José, he was not inclined to become angry or upset when we were not, at first, successful in catching Lucy with Andrew. Also, by getting José involved in the investigative process, we were able to get more accomplished and keep him satisfied. José was also essential in obtaining the secret address of Andrew's new residence, which was a critical link in cracking this case.

"Why Did My Wife Move to Gainesville?"

At the Holiday Inn, in the lounge, I was holding hands with Mr. Walter Bissell, a traveling salesman who appeared to have a lot of alcohol in him even though we had just arrived for the happy hour hors d'oeuvres. I ordered a glass of orange juice to accompany my potato skins and carrot sticks. Mr. Bissell ordered a couple of whiskeys on the rocks and began his story.

He had been married for 31 years. He was still very much in love with his wife, who was now in her mid-fifties. A number of years ago, his wife met a woman at the local country club and they became the best of friends. Last year, the friend's husband died. Now, suddenly, his wife, Barbie, decided to go live with her widowed best friend. Something was up, Mr. Bissell was convinced. He wanted me to find out everything, but he said the alimony was killing him. What could I do for a cheap, good price? Well, I told him he could purchase $50 worth of cosmetics for his wife and I could attempt to talk with her if she buys my story that she's my 100th customer and has just won $50 worth of free products. If not, we could try surveillance, but that would be much more costly and time consuming. Mr. Bissell said that he would pay for me to try speaking directly with his chatty, effervescent absent wife. I promised him I would do my best.

After completing the investigation, I met with Mr. Bissell once again at the Holiday Inn. This time, we sat inside a private banquet room where the staff had not yet cleaned up from the morning's meeting. We ate leftover cookies and drank sodas that remained in the melting ice. Before I turned the nine-page report over to Mr. Bissell, I warned him that he would not be happy with what he was about to read. We held hands again.

As he read the report, I noticed that his jaw was twitching. There were moments when he appeared as if he was about to cry. At other times, he balled up his fist, then would look at me and say, "She really didn't say that. You made this up, didn't you."

"No, Mr. Bissell. Why would I make this stuff up?"

He'd examine my face for a moment and then resumed reading the report.

Mr. Bissell left abruptly after reading the report. The next day he called me and accused me of being in cahoots with his wife. I told him that that was absurd. He called several more times to see if I had befriended his wife. In the end, I had to contact Mr. Bissell's attorney and explain to her that I wished to be left alone. I faxed her a letter to give to Mr. Bissell stating that the investigation was now completed and that if he wanted any additional information, he should contact another P.I. firm. I did not hear from Mr. Bissell anymore. I certainly hope he found peace and new love in his life.

Here's the report. Names of the people have been deleted to protect their privacy.

Angela V. Woodhull, Ph.D.
Po Box 14423
Gainesville, FL 32604
(352) 332-7746

RE: Conversation XXXXX
Date: XXXXX 1999

XXXXX stated that she is in the middle of a divorce but that she has rented her own apartment at XXXXX. No phone number as of yet. Will move in XXXXX 1999.

She is going to college for the first time in her life and plans to receive her AA Degree at XXXXX, with emphasis on becoming proficient as a medical transcriptionist. She is hoping that as part of her alimony settlement she will receive full tuition payment for the two years she plans to spend at XXXXX College, located in XXXXX. She had looked into becoming a court reporter but could not find a place of instruction in Gainesville; the nearest training center is Jacksonville and the course takes four years to complete. There is a course by mail but it seems too difficult. XXXXX College classes commence on XXXXX. It will take 18-21 months to graduate, with the Associate of Arts Degree.

XXXXX belongs to a singles' club; they meet at Rafferty's Restaurant. XXXXX indicated that she moved to Gainesville in XXXXX 1999. There seems to be a scarcity of available men in XXXXX club. XXXXX says she has not been attending the singles' club meetings but she just happened to be having supper with XXXXX one evening when a group of singles' club members came in and joined them.

XXXXX has been attending the monthly Chamber of Commerce mixers — $5 fee for non-Chamber members.

The next Chamber mixer will take place on Thursday evening, August 26, 1999. XXXXX speculated that it may take place somewhere in the Oaks Mall. XXXXX attended last month's Chamber mixer with XXXXX and some of XXXXX's girlfriends. It took place at a local radio station. They served good food, such as ribs and beef.

XXXXX is a XXXXX. She just had a birthday. For her birthday she went to Church Street in Orlando with XXXXX, et al. They went to Howl at the Moon (a sing-along piano bar), another place that is part of the Church Street attractions. There was a live band. They didn't get there until about 1 a.m. In attendance: XXXXX, XXXXX's son and his girlfriend, a girlfriend of XXXXX's who drove up from Clearwater, and XXXXX's boyfriend (who she met through XXXXX awhile back) — His name is XXXXX. XXXXX is 26. It surprised XXXXX very much to discover how many really young guys are attracted to older women these days. The "age thing" kinda bothers her but does not seem to bother XXXXX. In fact, XXXXX says that he is crazy about her and wants her to move in with him. But XXXXX said she has been married since she was 19 years old and she does not want to do that right now. XXXXX is a lot more mature than 26, according to XXXXX. He has a good job at the XXXXX, working as the manager of the XXXXX where a lot of restaurants are located. XXXXX likes to go out and dance with XXXXX and have a lot of fun. XXXXX is crazy about XXXXX too, but she again emphasized that she is reluctant to move in with him at this time.

When she is eighty, he will be only fifty — and so she is skeptical. They get along great except for times when XXXXX has an insecurity attack about the "age" thing. XXXXX is tall and thin with red hair, about XXXXX in height. XXXXX already has his college degree. Some of the restaurants in the XXXXX that he manages include XXXXX and XXXXX. XXXXX and XXXXX both work for XXXXX on campus — XXXXX met XXXXX through her friend, XXXXX, XXXXX, and XXXXX have been close friends for two years; in fact, mostly everyone thought that XXXXX and XXXXX were having an affair, but they weren't and have not. XXXXX and XXXXX go out together all the time. When XXXXX moved up in June, she started tagging along on the outings. XXXXX saw the movie "Stella Gets Her Groove Back," and she identified with the lead character, who is having an affair with a much younger man.

XXXXX's soon to be ex-husband and her two children live in Clearwater, FL. It's kind of a difficult time for XXXXX because XXXXX according to XXXXX, is trying to pull a lot of little sneaky things on her. He would like to have her back, but she is definitely not going back to him. XXXXX was physically abusive at times a while back. XXXXX's kids are now grown and raised, so it's time for a transition. XXXXX also alleged that XXXXX "ran around" a lot on her during the 31-year marriage. She stayed over the years for the sake of the children. XXXXX could not understand why she wanted to leave. She told XXXXX it was because she was sick of him and didn't love him anymore. All of her friends cheered her on and said "You Go, Girl," and they felt that her leaving was long past overdue. There were problems throughout the marriage, as early as the first three months of the marriage. There is no way in hell she would ever go back. She would rather have to go out and work three jobs than go back to Mr. XXXXX. She wishes she had left 28 years ago. But at 19 she felt she knew it all; now, she looks back and feels she knew nothing.

Last year, when XXXXX's husband died (her and XXXXX have been best friends for 25 years.) XXXXX knew how miserable XXXXX had been over the years. And she had grown increasingly miserable. So, one weekend, after her husband's death, XXXXX said to XXXXX that she did not have to go back home. She could move in with XXXXX XXXXX. XXXXX blames XXXXX for XXXXX's leaving — he thinks it is entirely XXXXX's fault. XXXXX started going to Gainesville every weekend because it was the only place where she could keep her sanity.

XXXXX still lives at home with XXXXX, he is 25. He's going to school; he has emotional problems; he doesn't hold down a job. XXXXX, the daughter, lives with her boyfriend. The children are being somewhat supportive of their mother at this point, but XXXXX fears that they will withdraw their support when they find out their mother is dating a man who is only one year older than her son. At this point only XXXXX's sister, nephew and the nephew's fiancée know about the affair with XXXXX. XXXXX is trying his best to find out what is going on. In fact, he's gone so far as to have XXXXX subpoenaed at work. They want to put her on the witness stand, the excuse being to ask if XXXXX is paying any rent or part of the utilities. She has been paying zero to XXXXX. But XXXXX's lawyer told her to get out and get her own place because once they have XXXXX on the witness stand they can brutalize her with questions about <u>any</u> subject. Now that XXXXX is moving out, she is hoping that her attorney can get XXXXX's testimony cancelled. Her attorney is going to claim that it is irrelevant since Florida is a no-fault divorce state. But there are no guarantees. XXXXX claims that XXXXX wants to know so that he can have an excuse to go haywire (if he finds out about XXXXX) because he is a "crazy man." He could be violent. XXXXX hid out for two weeks when she first left. She waited for XXXXX to calm down. Then they talked. But when he finds out about XXXXX oh, boy! XXXXX met XXXXX two years ago — a long time before anything transpired between them. In fact, XXXXX and XXXXX would sometimes spend the weekends in Clearwater at XXXXX's house. But nothing was transpiring between XXXXX and XXXXX at that time except for simple friendship. XXXXX met XXXXX at that time. In fact, on the day that XXXXX met XXXXX the four of them went out dancing that evening. That evening, riding in a car with XXXXX, XXXXX told XXXXX about all of his extra-curricular girlfriends. XXXXX told XXXXX about girlfriends he had in the Carolinas. XXXXX even related their names to XXXXX. XXXXX then related the conversation to XXXXX, and XXXXX told XXXXX. XXXXX wondered at that time why XXXXX would be "stupid" enough to reveal these things to XXXXX, since XXXXX knew that XXXXX and XXXXX were such good friends and that XXXXX and XXXXX were best friends.

On another occasion, XXXXX came to Clearwater for the weekend with a guy she was dating and that guy brought along one of his male friends. The five of them went out that evening. That evening at the bar, XXXXX said to XXXXX's friend's friend that he XXXXX was checking the bar for all the prettiest women and he had spotted the prettiest woman. The conclusion? XXXXX's friend felt sorry for XXXXX and felt it would be quite justified if XXXXX did anything. Here was XXXXX talking about other women in the bar to a man he had just met. XXXXX said this was XXXXX's nature all throughout the marriage. Conclusion: XXXXX feels she is so much better off without XXXXX.

The first time XXXXX and XXXXX had sex (about a month ago), XXXXX felt scared. She thought to herself, "What in the world am I doing!?" But the sex was real hot. She thought she had lost her mind. (Figuratively, of course, not literally.) At first, she told him not to look at her. She would turn off all the lights and jump under the covers, but since those first few encounters, she has stopped being this inhibited. XXXXX gets credit for making XXXXX feel so comfortable. (This has been going on for "a month or so.") XXXXX is described as a "real sweetheart." He has dated older women in the past. He has informed his mom, his dad, and all of his friends about his romantic relationship with XXXXX. One weekend, XXXXX's mom came to visit and went out with XXXXX and XXXXX. XXXXX would love to move in with XXXXX. He would move in with her "in a minute," but XXXXX is not going to ask him. In fact, XXXXX has really been pushing the issue, but it is "too soon" for XXXXX being that she is coming out from a tumultuous 31-year marriage. To jump right into another serious relationship just feels a bit much. In fact, XXXXX doubts that she will ever marry again. XXXXX is crazy about kids. XXXXX has pointed out that she is past the age of bearing children, but XXXXX's in love, says "he doesn't care." XXXXX's mother told XXXXX that she has never seen her son so happy.

XXXXX says her relationship with XXXXX is highly unusual in that she has never, in her entire life, had a relationship with someone that is so all encompassing. She can talk to XXXXX about anything — any subject. They do everything together and they both have a lot in common. They like different types of music; if they go out dancing, they'll negotiate, spending half the night at his kind of place and half the night at her kind of place. XXXXX loves country line dancing. XXXXX at first, would just sit and watch, but XXXXX has taught XXXXX a couple of dances. The couple recently spent four days together down in Key West. He loves when they are out in public or in a bar to constantly show public displays of affection — constantly kissing her face and holding her hand. This is all new for XXXXX. She has never been with such a demonstrative man before. XXXXX's husband wasn't openly affectionate even during their courtship prior to their marriage. XXXXX is a romantic. One day he sent XXXXX a dozen red roses, just for the heck of it. The message on the card: "I Love You." For her birthday, he bought her a single red rose and some sexy lingerie from Victoria's Secret. XXXXX's daughter et al. knows about the romantic affair. For awhile, XXXXX was still wearing her diamond engagement ring on her right hand, but when XXXXX indicated that it bothered him, XXXXX stopped wearing any of her wedding rings. Every time he was holding her hand, he would check out the diamond, so one day XXXXX asked him if it bothered him. When he said "yes," she stopped wearing it.

XXXXX knows that XXXXX is currently going though a divorce. He has heard some wild stories of things XXXXX has done over the years and XXXXX thinks it's pretty awful. One night XXXXX said, "I don't have anything against XXXXX except that he must have lost his mind to have let you slip through his fingers."

XXXXX doesn't know if XXXXX is dating. She doesn't know and she doesn't care.

XXXXX's secret of staying thin (even though she claims to have gained a little weight lately). She used to walk a lot. She holds off on eating breakfast and lunch. Has perhaps a salad for supper. XXXXX filed for divorce on June 13. Moved to Gainesville June 15. Her whole life she has watched what she eats.

XXXXX where she is moving to, has a really nice workout room. So far, she has not a stitch of furniture. Nothing has been divided as of yet. Her apartment is a two bedroom, two bath. On XXXXX is taking two full days of classes on computers at XXXXX. On the XXXXX, and XXXXX she will be attending a wedding — her nephew is getting married in Clearwater. She hopes to get some furniture at that time. XXXXX has not been invited to the wedding, but XXXXX's two children will be present. XXXXX starts on XXXXX but she is thinking of going with XXXXX to Kentucky to see the Gator Game. She might get a part-time day job in September and then attend classes at XXXXX college at night. This week she plans to get a telephone in her new apartment, an unlisted number. That way she doesn't have to listen to XXXXX. XXXXX was wearing a blue bathing suit with black jogging shorts. Her hair was pinned up. She was about to use a machine to clean the cement driveway. She said that her attorney told her not to work for now.

END OF REPORT

Backseat Action

A man wanted proof that his wife was cheating. For this job, we used four investigators and three vehicles. First, we followed the wife to her lover's place of work. The two of them then entered his vehicle and headed to the upstairs level of a lonely parking garage. We followed the couple to the top level, then one of our investigators stepped out with a briefcase, so that the couple believed that no one was inside our vehicle. As soon as our cohort entered the elevator, the couple began undressing. This was one of those great occasions when we videotaped live sex as it occurred.

When the couple finished, they re-dressed and headed down, out of the parking garage. Little did they know that another vehicle at the ground level was also in the process of filming them as they exited the parking garage. In other words, the entire episode was captured on film. I don't think you could say our client was "delighted" with the results, but he certainly got his money's worth.

Points to Remember: What made this investigation a success?

1. **Several vehicles were needed** to pull off this investigation.

2. **The vehicle that followed the couple up to the top level of the parking garage appeared to be empty.** When our investigator reached the bottom level, he simply joined our other investigator (the one who followed the couple out of the parking garage).

3. **Two vehicles with walkie-talkies are always needed** to follow someone in traffic. By leap-frogging each other in traffic, the subject rarely suspects that he is being followed.

Who is Connie?

A woman said she knew her husband was cheating; she had listened in to their private little phone chats on several occasions on the home extension line. She had heard them laughing and giggling about her, making fun of her. Now she wanted to meet Connie directly. She had a couple of phone numbers. Could I find out where Connie works and take her along?

After making a few phone calls, asking directly for Connie, I discovered that Connie Reese works as a student loan officer for the University of Florida. It just so happened that the new semester was about to begin. I called the local student newspaper and asked them if I could freelance a story about the student loan office. They were delighted to have me offer them a great and timely story.

I called my client. "Are you ready to go meet Connie?" Suddenly, she had cold feet. Since I personally know this woman, I knew she was not about to do any bodily harm to Connie. In fact, she had lived in silent suffering with her cheating spouse for 35 years. After much cajoling, I picked up Arlene and we went down to the student loan office with our notepads and cameras. Here we were: two grown women posing as first year undergraduate journalism students looking to write a story for the campus newspaper. After interviewing several of the student loan staff about the ups and downs of processing all the student loans at the hectic beginning of a semester, we were finally invited to go speak with Connie.

Connie sat in her office eating cheese crackers and sipping a diet soda. The first thing that struck me about Connie was the striking resemblance between her and my client/friend. It was as though Arlene were suddenly 15 years younger and

20 pounds thinner (although both women are on the heavy-set side with similar hair-dos and similar gestures — and their laughs are *identical!*).

We sat there for about 45 minutes just talking in general and also about student loans with Connie while sharing her cheese crackers and sipping on sodas. I was surprised at how well Arlene remained composed. Connie was so friendly, she even provided us with her home phone number so we could continue the interview, if necessary.

After leaving her office, we checked the city directory and obtained her home address. Next, we drove past her residence. Connie had just arrived home from work, and guess whose car was sitting in her driveway? You guessed it! I told Arlene to go ahead to the door and confront her cheating spouse. She did not have the nerve.

Instead, she went home, got on the Internet, and located her high school sweetheart, who was in the process of going through his third divorce. The two of them fell back in love, and within six months, Arlene had divorced her cheating husband and was happily married to her first sweetheart.

Incidentally, Connie dumped Arlene's ex-husband for another man.

Date at the Gym

A woman contacted me because she believed her boyfriend of eight years was cheating on her.

"He spends four hours a night working out at the gym. **Nobody** spends four hours a night at the gym. Can you go find out what he does?"

And so I dressed up in my "I'm ready for anything" look and headed for the gym.

The first night, when I spotted my subject, I just watched from afar without approaching him. He, indeed, spent many hours working out at the gym with what appeared to be a good buddy and the buddy's girlfriend. I wasn't quite sure, at first, who the woman was with, but by the second night, I had a wealth of information.

During my second visit to the gym, I knew Herman's routine. First, he would warm up for 20 minutes on the bicycles. It was during this time that I rode a stationary bike next to his and struck up a chatty, flirty conversation with him.

"Wow! You look **so much** like my ex-boyfriend! He's also Afro-American and he's from Atlanta. I just moved down here to go to college and I don't know anybody."

"Well, you now know me," Herman said. And he extended a hand.

We talked for a while, chatting about Gainesville, football, the weather, my major, his life, all that kind of stuff, and then he invited me to join him and his two friends for a **real** workout on the free weights side of the gym. I told him I had never lifted weights. He promised to show me how and said I would be an expert in no time.

His friends, Kendra and Shawn, were really nice people. They took a liking to me instantly and welcomed me as a fourth member of their team. Afterwards, they invited me out for ice cream, but I said I had to get going.

On the third day, I met up with Herman and his friends at the gym. This time, he asked me out on a date. I said, "But a guy as good-looking as you must already have a woman."

"I do have a woman, but we don't get along. We've been living together for eight years, and we have a child, but there is no more romance."

"But don't you have any other girlfriends? Ah, come on."

He assured me that there was no one else. His friends egged me to come along that night and go dancing. After all, I was new in town and had few friends.

I called my client and asked permission to go dancing. She called off the investigation immediately.

"In other words, what you're telling me is that he ain't cheating, but he would **like** to cheat."

"Yep. That sounds about right."

That night, she had a rageful confrontation with Herman. "That woman was **not** interested in you in the **least!**" she shouted. "She is a P.I. and I hired her to spy on you!"

Herman was equally furious, natch.

The investigation was complete and I prayed that I'd never run into Herman and his friends ever again. (By the way, I really **did** like them!)

At the Christmas Party

A man in his mid-forties contacted me. He was upset because his wife of nine years had suddenly left him and moved in with a girlfriend she had recently acquired at her new job. During the first eight years of their marriage, Candy had stayed home as a housewife. Suddenly, she was interested in employment and then, two weeks after taking her job as a secretary for a pest control company, she split. My client, Don, wanted to know what was going on. Was she dating? Had she become a lesbian? Was there a boyfriend? Candy had given no explanation when she abruptly departed and Don was under the impression that their marriage had been solid. Now, Candy would not even speak to him. And Don had no idea where Candy was staying. Right before splitting, Candy did manage to have Don buy her a brand new car. He paid cash in full for the vehicle. The next day, she was gone.

My strategy was to follow her from work on Friday evening and see where she goes. Arriving about 4:30 p.m. on a Friday in mid-December, I circled the parking lot looking for her brand new vehicle. Meanwhile, I.J. parked in a lot across the street with a video camera, a tape recorder (for recording license plate numbers and descriptions of people who exit the building), and a pair of binoculars.

As I drove around the building and through the parking lot, however, I was struck by good luck, as usual. (I don't know why, but good luck usually is with me in the P.I. business.) It just so happened that the pest control company was hosting their annual Christmas party for employees and guests. A man clad in cowboy clothes and a Texas-style cowboy hat approached me as I circled the parking lot.

"May I help you?"

"Ah, I'm looking for Brian." (I made up a name on the spot.)

"You mean Brian from our Tallahassee office?"

"Yeah!" (What else could I say at this point?)

"I didn't know he was coming down for our annual Christmas party."

"I'm sorry. He wanted it to be a surprise. I hope he's not mad at me for telling you."

"I won't say a word."

"Actually, he wasn't quite sure if he'd be coming or not. If he doesn't show up, am I still invited?"

"Of course. Park anywhere over there. The party will start in about twenty minutes."

I went back and informed I.J. about my streak of good luck. I had pictures of Candy with me. Now, I could observe her throughout the night and report back to my client her every move. If she should leave the party, I.J. was prepared to follow her. He had spotted her vehicle in the parking lot.

Sure enough, about 20 minutes later, the employees came outside and starting helping themselves to the hors d'oeuvres and the drinks. I helped myself, too, struck up a conversation with a couple of guys, and managed to sit with them at their table. I told everyone I was waiting on Brian and I prayed that Brian would never show up or be contacted by phone about me. However, I was prepared, just in case he did show up. I would feign surprise and say it was **another** Brian I was looking for and there must be some kind of mistake. In fact, I am so ditzy, I must have gone to the wrong pest control company. Anyway, Brian never did show up, so I was safe, and I blended in well with the crowd.

Soon, I spotted Candy. She appeared to be much thinner than the woman in the picture. She wore her hair in a long, curly perm, dyed blonde, with a poodle bang in the front. She was with three other women. All of them appeared to be in their mid-thirties. All of them had identical dyed blonde poodle hairstyles, and all of them were clad in black jeans, black t-shirts, and black boots. When one of them got up from the table to go use the bathroom, the other three would tag along. When the DJ came an hour later, the four of them danced provocatively with many of the pest control men. Periodically, the four women would go off into the far corner of the parking lot with some of the guys. Watching out of the corner of my eye, I saw that they were passing around a joint. This behavior continued for several hours.

A group of guys huddled together talking at the back of a pick-up truck invited me to join their conversation. Within a few minutes, I was inquiring about the four girls.

"Oh, them!" said one. "Boy, they got quite a reputation. You don't want to be hanging out with them girls. They sleep with anybody. Go to Big Daddy's Lounge every Friday night, pick up different guys, then they brag about their weekend affairs on Monday mornings. I wouldn't touch any of them with a ten-foot pole. One of them is still married. She left her old man because she was bored and wanted to have a good time."

Around 10 p.m., the girls left. I.J. followed Candy home to a trailer park and jotted down the number of the trailer. The next day, I called the office and said I had a package to deliver to that trailer but I couldn't make out the name on the label. Thus, I found out the name of the owner of the trailer and it was, indeed, her coworker.

When I shared the information with Don, he was, at first, flabbergasted. A week later, he called me back and said he had made peace with the information. He was no longer hoping and waiting for Candy to come back. He was ready to file for a divorce.

Points to Remember: What made this investigation a success?

1. **Luck.** This was a case of "being in the right place at the right time." If the annual Christmas party were not taking place on that particular evening, I would not have found out so much information so easily. However, there was another way to obtain information. If I had followed Candy to Big Daddy's Lounge, I'm sure I could have written a report on her behavior at the bar. Also, since this is a known hangout for pest control employees, I still might have been able to talk to some guys who were familiar with Candy (and her girlfriends') reputations.

2. **Quick thinking.** It turns out that the man in the 10-gallon hat was the owner of the pest control company. By thinking fast, I was able to invite myself to the party without him becoming suspicious. (By the way, I found

out, during the course of the evening, that Brian is the owner's nephew.)

3. **I.J. was also a critical part of this investigation.** At one point, he climbed the roof of a nearby building and captured Candy on tape dancing provocatively with several men.

You're a Winner!

A Jeff Lutz contacted me by phone and wanted to know if I could find out who owned the cell phone number that was continuously appearing on his itemized statement. Last month's records indicated that the number had been dialed 78 times, though his wife claimed she had no idea to whom the number belonged. Lutz said a man always answered the number but the receiver would simply hang up when he asked him to identify himself.

"Let me have the number, please," I said. "I'll call you back in 10 minutes."

Sure enough, ten minutes later, I called Mr. Lutz and gave him the name, home address, work address, make and model of the man's pickup truck, and directions to his country home trailer. Here's what I did:

"Hello."

"Congratulations! This is radio station KZK FM and you have just won two free tickets to opening night of *Star Wars!!*"

"Hot damn!" the man replied. "I **knew** this was going to be my lucky day!"

"Now, all I need to know is the complete spelling of your name, your address, how to find you, etc., and if our van doesn't get there this evening, your work address."

The man turned over all the information without asking a single question.

When I re-contacted Mr. Lutz with the information I assured him, "Mr. Lutz, if you're worried that your wife may be having an affair with this fellow, don't fret too much. It's apparent that the man greatly lacks in intelligence, so I'm sure the affair will not last long."

Last I heard, the man was still sitting by his phone waiting for his two free *Star Wars* tickets.

Do Used Car Salesmen Cheat on Their Wives?

A distraught looking Afro-American woman met with me to discuss her husband, whom she believed was cheating on her.

"He's been coming home very late at night," Ruby Archer said, "claiming that he has to deliver cars directly to clients' homes late at night. I just get the feeling that something is going on."

Mrs. Archer paid me for one ten-hour day of investigative services. Meanwhile, she told her husband that she would be going to their beach condo for the next few days. That way, he would be free to do whatever he wanted during that time period.

The Double Whammy Approach

To obtain a complete picture of what Mr. Tray Archer might be doing with his time besides selling used cars, we used a two-investigator approach. (1) I dressed up in my best "I'm-ready-for-anything, baby" outfit (skin tight black leather pants, a skimpy black halter top with my black bra straps showing, a black leather jacket, and high, high heels, hair combed straight down with a side bang covering one eye, and lots of dark red lipstick) and headed for the used car lot to "buy a car." (2) I.J. kept a watchful eye from his vehicle and was ready to follow Mr. Archer no matter where he might go.

Prior to heading out for Fred's Fine Used Cars, I did a brief background investigation on Mr. Archer and discovered that he used to work as the assistant manager of Big Ben's Supermarket. I then remembered that I had had a run-in with him about seven years ago. I had been purchasing all of my groceries at Big Ben's, except for soymilk, which I purchased from the local health food store. The price of soymilk at Big Ben's was much higher than the health food store's, so I reasoned with one of the Big Ben managers that he should sell me the soymilk at the health food store price and he agreed to give me the discounted price. However, one day Mr. Archer was on duty and when he saw that the cashier was giving me the soymilk at a reduced price, he halted this practice. I was very upset with him — to the point that I contacted the corporate office, but received no satisfaction. The result? I stopped shopping at Big Ben's and have never been back. Now, this happened seven years ago. Really, it was not that big of a deal, but other, nicer supermarkets have been erected in my neighborhood since that time, so I simply have not shopped there any more. Now, there is a reason why I am relating this rather lame story, as it ended up working well as part of my pretext for the day. Read on!

I also learned from two other persons who had worked with Mr. Archer when he was assistant manager at Big Ben's that he was quite a flirtatious guy, especially with Afro-American women. One man told me that Mr. Archer carried around a personal cell phone and that he was constantly on the phone chatting with a variety of his women friends. It was also rumored that Mr. Archer associated with brothers who sell drugs and deal in prostitution. I was anxious to see how Mr. Archer would treat me if I paid him a visit at the used car lot.

I called Mr. Archer at Fred's Fine Used Cars prior to visiting with Mr. Archer in person. I told him that I remembered him from Big Ben's Supermarket and that he had come highly recommended as a fine salesman. "But I usually don't trust used car salesmen," I told him. "I require a lot of attention, Mr. Archer. Will you pay a lot of attention to me?"

"Why, sure, ma'am," he said. "Come on down."

At the Car Lot

I arrived at Fred's Fine Used Cars at approximately 2 p.m. Mr. Archer was busy assisting other customers. The front desk paged him and said he had a guest in the lobby. About 20 minutes later, Tray Archer introduced himself to me and offered me a soda. He escorted me to his office area and said he would be back shortly. Meanwhile, I paged through his personal book, which included testimonials from past satisfied customers, Biblical quotes, prayers, and a certificate announcing that Mr. Archer was also a part-time minister. Now, a man of the cloth should certainly be monogamous, no doubt, so I simply observed Mr. Archer while he interacted with other customers. He was presently assisting a 19-year-old college woman who had just purchased a brand new Mustang. She told me, while she was waiting for her temp tag, that Mr. Archer had been very nice to her and very professional.

Another hour passed and Mr. Archer had still not assisted me. Finally, he came over to the table where I was sitting, sipping on a 7-Up, and told me that he was too busy to help me but he would hook me up with another salesman who could show me around the lot. I told him it was only him whom I wanted to deal with. I did look at one car with another salesman. During the ride, I asked him about Mr.

Archer's reputation for being a flirt. He said that he flirts with everyone but never remembers him leaving the lot with any woman.

Three hours passed and Mr. Archer was finally ready to take me out and show me a couple of vehicles. But first, he wanted to run a credit check on me. I told him that I didn't have much credit. I then called one of my partners, D.H., and posed as his cousin.

"Hi, cuz, it's me," I said. "I'm down here at Fred's Fine Used Cars and I need to buy a vehicle. Will you co-sign for me?"

D.H. agreed to be a co-signer, so I filled out the paperwork using his name. It was now nearly 6:30 and Mr. Archer and I finally took a stroll around the lot in search of a used car that might suit my needs. We decided to take a Voyager mini-van out for a test drive.

During the ride, I did everything possible to try to get Mr. Archer interested in me. I told him I had fallen in love with him, that I needed a ride home because I was without a vehicle (in truth, I had parked 10 blocks down the road), and that I preferred to date black men, especially black married men because I wasn't interested in anything real serious — just some fun. Mr. Archer did not bite the bait at all.

I then decided it would be best to become a type of crazy lady who would not give up or take a hint. During the ride I gunned the car several times, then would slam on the brakes. Mr. Archer became somewhat frightened of me and asked me to take him back to the car dealership.

It was now approximately 7:30 p.m. and I needed a reason to stay at the car dealership even though Mr. Archer was no longer interested in showing me additional vehicles. He said that he got off work at 8 p.m. and he needed the half hour to complete his paperwork. I told him that I needed a ride home. He attempted to find me an alternative ride home, but

I refused. Instead, I dialed a friend to come pick me up, which was really my own office number. The number rang and rang. No one picked up. (Of course.) Every ten minutes or so I kept dialing the number, telling Mr. Archer that I was sure my friend would be home shortly and would give me a ride.

While Mr. Archer completed his paperwork, I paced the floor in front of him and then finally joined him at his worktable. I leaned forward and said to him, "Tray, maybe you don't remember me, but I remember you. In fact, we had a big fight seven years ago. And I've never forgotten that fight. Do you remember me, Tray?"

"No, ma'am," he replied, continuing to complete his paperwork while he ignored me.

"Well, back when you were the assistant manager of Big Ben's, I used to buy soymilk there at a discounted price. One day, you put an end to all that. Do you remember that, Tray?"

"No, ma'am." He continued to write, his head down, ignoring me.

"Well, I've never ever forgotten that day, Tray. You changed my life. Here, I had been getting soymilk at a very reasonable price. But you changed that. You changed the course of my life forever on that day. And today, I came here, hoping that you'd make it up to me in some way, but you haven't. You haven't at all. So, we still have a score to settle, don't we."

Mr. Archer continued to write. The seven-year soymilk grudge was so ludicrous that it was all I could do to keep from laughing. But the story was legitimate and there was a good chance that he did, in fact, remember the incident. This story did two things for me: (1) It gave me a legitimate reason to linger at the car lot and see if any woman came to pick him up at 8 p.m. when he got off of work; (2) Mr. Archer was definitely concluding — from the way I had driven the Voyager — and the way I was currently talking, that I was a crazy lady who was there stalking him. In fact, I'm surprised he didn't ask his boss to have me removed from the premises.

By 8:30, Mr. Archer headed out the door and drove off in an old blue Chevrolet. At this point, I.J., who had been watching him all day, took over and followed him. Mr. Archer did, indeed, go straight home.

We lingered out on the street for a few hours in a hidden spot to see if Mr. Archer was going to go back out anywhere but he did not exit his home.

At midnight, I called his home phone. He did pick up the phone and there seemed to be no one else present except for Mr. Archer.

The following day, I spoke with his wife and told her what had happened. "I think you frightened him," she said. "He slept with a gun next to his pillow all that night."

On the ride home, I replayed the soymilk get-back in my head. I laughed so hard that there were tears coming out of my eyes. There was no evidence on this day that Mr. Archer has been or is cheating on his wife, but perhaps the soymilk stalker put enough fear in him that he won't try any hanky panky with anyone in the near future.

But I Still Love Her!

Dale Victor was in his last semester of law school. Soon, he would be taking his final tests and preparing for the Bar examination. It seemed as though a rosy future should be facing him. Instead, he sat inside his expensive two-bedroom apartment, located close to the law school, with all the blinds closed. There was trash, dirty clothes, and broken furniture everywhere. A skinny cat roamed the floor, frequently meowing. On his coffee table, an ashtray was overflowing with cigarette butts, some of which had spilled onto the table and carpet. Dale had not shaved in several days. There were heavy black circles and bags under his eyes. His breath reeked of Jack Daniels vomit.

We sat in his dark living room together, holding hands. Tears continuously streamed down Dale's face.

"I want her back!" Dale sobbed. "My wife left me two months ago, and I just don't understand! I gave her everything she wanted! I gave her money! I gave her all the freedom she wanted! She said I was controlling, but I wasn't. I even let her go out with other guys. She said they were just platonic friends, so I believed her! Why did she leave me!?"

Dale could not speak at the moment. His tears were flowing uncontrollably. I arose from the sofa and searched for a box of Kleenex tissues. But all I could find was a roll of toilet paper on the kitchen floor next to the empty cat food bowl.

Dale blew his nose loudly and then took a swig of his cold, black coffee.

"I want you to find out if there's another man. She says she still loves me, but she won't come back to me."

"Are you still supporting her?"

"Yes. She was just over here two nights ago and I gave her $300. I'm a nice guy. I really am!!" The tears and sobs began again. "I love her! Why won't she come back to me?"

The Strategy

After listening to Dale for more than two hours, I decided that the best and quickest strategy to gain the information Dale wanted would be to talk directly with Jolane. Dale told me she worked at a novelty gift shop at the mall. For this assignment, I took along an intern who posed as my pregnant daughter.

At The Mall

It was easy to spot Jolane at the gift shop. Just like in the photos Dale had lent me, Jolane was a beautiful young woman with long blonde hair and blue eyes. She was chatting with a coworker when "my pregnant daughter" and I approached the gift stand.

"Is there anything I can help you with today?" Jolane asked us.

"Yes!" I began. "My daughter is two months pregnant and we want to plan a baby shower for her. Something unique. We'd like to buy party favors with a Gator theme because her fiancé attends Florida State in Tallahassee, so there's always this competition between them."

"Oh, that sounds cute and different!" Jolane said.

"Do you have any suggestions? We've never done anything like this before."

Jolane pointed to several items that she thought might work. We walked around the little gift shop, feigning interest in all of the tawdry paraphernalia.

"Listen, I'm not really quite sure what I want to purchase. You wouldn't happen to know anything about party planning, would you?"

"Well, yes, in fact, I do!" Jolane beamed. "I did some party planning for a couple of conferences when I lived in California!"

"Oh, that sounds marvelous!" I declared. "How much would you charge me if I just simply turned this project over to you and let you design the party games, buy the supplies, the party favors, and just organize everything?"

"Oh, I wouldn't charge you anything," Jolane said, smiling.

"Oh, I couldn't do that! This is going to be a big job. I am prepared to pay you $200 to be my baby shower party consultant. Is it a deal?"

Jolane's big blue eyes lit up. "Sure! I'm kinda broke right now. I would do it for free — honestly! But if you're offering to pay me..."

As we spoke, the phone at Jolane's novelty gift shop rang on six occasions. "It's for you!" her partner kept saying, as he handed her the phone repeatedly. Each time she took the call, she said, "I'm busy with a customer right now. Can I call you back in a little bit?" She showed no signs of exasperation. Finally, by the sixth call, I said, "Boy, you certainly are popular!"

"Oh, it's just my ex-boyfriend calling again. I broke up with him a few months ago and he still can't get over it."

Jolane and I arranged to meet on Thursday on the University of Florida campus at a mega-Gator novelty gift shop that would certainly meet all of my party needs.

Living in Hell

Dale had a very hard time waiting until Thursday to find out what was going on with Jolane and their relationship. He called me repeatedly. He called her repeatedly. He sounded like a broken record, asking me incessantly if I thought she still loved him and if she's going to come back.

Dale had not been attending any of his law school classes. There was a good chance he was not going to pass this final semester. Prior to Thursday, as we spoke, I tried to prepare him for the worst. From what I had witnessed already, Jolane was moving on. She did not appear to be grieving over Dale nor did it appear that she was missing him in the least. I gently and diplomatically explained these facts to Dale, but he certainly felt it was just a matter of time before she would return. He believed he would just have to be patient. Meanwhile, he laid on his couch, smoked hundreds of cigarettes, and ate canned tuna.

At the Gator Gift Shop

Jolane had taken her job as "baby shower party consultant" very seriously. She greeted me with a notebook turned open to twelve pages she had meticulously hand written — an outline that included a list of party favors, snack foods, how to write up the invitations, and games we could play. I told her I was very hungry, that I had not eaten all day, and would she mind if I got a bite to eat before we browsed the party shop. "Oh, sure. No problem," she said. "I'm kind of hungry myself."

Inside the Orange and Brew, we snacked on salads and nachos with cheese sauce.

Jolane turned her notebook to the section she had written on baby shower party games. "This one I particularly like," she said. "You give everyone a 4 oz. baby bottle to suck on. The first one who finishes wins."

"Oh, that's pretty funny," I said.

Another game involved blindfolding the volunteers and having them taste various kinds of chocolate candy bars to see if they could identify them. Little did they know, the chocolates they were tasting had been heated and then mashed into the seats of baby diapers. While the contestants smelled and licked the diaper contents, a videographer would document the event, while onlookers laugh hysterically.

Truly, Jolane was on the ball. I was impressed with her work. And if I ever did host a baby shower, I certainly would use her notes.

Sipping on iced tea, I said to her, "Jolane, I have some pretty bad news for you. In fact, I'm very upset today. In fact, I don't think we're going to be buying any party favors today."

Jolane looked truly concerned. "What happened?"

I laid my head in my arms on the table. "You certainly don't have time or interest in hearing all of my problems."

"Oh, no, go ahead. I don't mind listening at all. In fact, I have a few problems of my own right now."

"You do? Well, maybe I can listen to you, too. But first, let me tell you my problem."

I then told Jolane that my daughter confessed to me last evening that she's not quite sure who the father is of the child. It might not be her fiancé. Therefore, the Gator theme might not even work. She wanted to wait until having a blood test before having any kind of shower.

"Oh, that's awful!" Jolane said. "You must be devastated!"

"I am," I said, and I almost broke into tears.

Soon, Jolane was telling me all about the nightmare of living with Dale. She had met him at a party. He seemed like a nice guy. Shortly thereafter, she moved in with him. Within a few weeks, he had become a control freak, monitoring her comings and goings, not even allowing her to see her parents more than once a week. She was permitted to have only two phone calls per day. Dale would not allow her to work. He wanted her to stay home so he could have full control over her. In order to move out, she had to call a girlfriend, wait for Dale to go to school, and then leave as quickly as possible. Dale came home unexpectedly as the two girls were hauling off things in the trunks of their cars. Dale panicked and pinned Jolane to the bedroom wall. Jolane's girlfriend contacted the police. Charges were pressed against both of them. Dale was charged with battery and kidnapping. Dale claimed that he was battered by Jolane.

Jolane felt that the state prosecuting attorney's office would be dropping the charges against her. Meanwhile, her family hired an attorney who was in the process of attempting to negotiate an out of court settlement between Dale and

Jolane. Jolane's family said they would drop the charges against Dale (which could terminate his law career, if the charges remained) if he would agree to stop contacting and stalking Jolane.

Yes, Jolane was seeing another man. Shortly after leaving Dale, she ran into an old boyfriend who's now stationed in the military in Greensboro, N.C. They began e-mailing and calling one another. He's planning on meeting her in Jacksonville in a few weeks. Jolane plans to attend a fashion design school in North Carolina where she will be closer to Michael, but her career plans come first. If it doesn't work out with Michael, she will continue school.

If Dale doesn't stop bothering her, she may even move to England because her father has dual citizenship and this is an option for his offspring. Jolane (and I'm sure this won't surprise you) has no intentions of ever returning to Dale. According to Jolane, they were never even married. He was simply a weird boyfriend she had for less than six months.

Back at the dungeon

"Does she still love me?" Dale wanted to know. There were chocolate candy wrappers all over the coffee table. A few dead roaches lay on the table next to a can of Raid. Dale chewed his fingernails and eyeballed me intensely. "Did she talk to you? Did she tell you anything?" Dale had been very skeptical about my approach to this case. He did not believe that Jolane would open up to a perfect stranger.

I examined Dale's sorrowful face. Panning his trashed apartment, I decided to make a suggestion. "Come on, Dale. You've been living like this for two months. Let's clean up this place."

"No. I can't," he wailed. "I'm too depressed. Besides, I like my bat cave just the way it is," he protested.

"Then let's go for a walk around the parking lot."

"No. I can't! I feel too weak."

I grabbed a jacket off of a nearby chair. "Here. Put this on. We're going for a walk."

"She's Gone"

We walked around the parking lot about six times, arm and arm, like two lovers. As we walked, I slowly broke the news to my client. I told him everything. He was handling the news better than I thought ...until I asked him, "Why did you lie to me? Why did you tell me you were married?"

Dale became ballistic. He pulled away from my arm and marched back into the bat cave.

"Here!" he shouted, flinging a set of legal-size papers at me. "If we weren't married, then what is this!?"

I quickly scanned the divorce papers and looked up at Dale, speechless.

"You see! She's a little liar! A little liar! I never tried to control her! She made up everything!!"

While we spoke, there was a knock on the door. It was a deputy sheriff with a subpoena for Dale. Glancing at the new set of court papers, Dale seemed to be suddenly completely over Jolane.

"Oh, no!" he gasped. "My ex-wife has found me again. If I don't pay $2,500 in back child support by the end of this week, she's putting my ass in jail!"

I was astounded. "Your ex-wife?"

"Yeah. I was married for seven years. We have two kids, ages five and three, a boy and a girl. She moved to Columbia and now she still wants to pursue me for child support." Dale grabbed a fistful of his hair. "Jeez! I can't believe this is happening to me!"

I left Dale with his two sets of court papers. A week later, I called him, just to see how he was doing. The recording said his number had been disconnected.

But I Still Love Her! — II

Conrad sat Indian-style on my office floor, crying, holding my hands.

"My wife of 31 years left me two months ago and moved back in with her parents. But I still love her! I love this woman! I really, truly love her!" Conrad sighed deeply and bowed his head. Tears streamed down his face. He looked up at me. "You don't know how much I love this woman. God, I love this woman. I would do anything to get her back."

Conrad removed a photo from his wallet. "Look at her. Isn't she beautiful? God, I love this woman."

"So, what happened? Why did she leave?" I inquired.

"I don't know," Conrad confessed. There were a few beats of silence.

"They say I was violent toward her, but I wasn't! I love this woman! I would never hurt her in any way!" More tears streamed down his face. I handed him a Kleenex. He blew his nose.

"Who's 'they'? Who said you were violent?"

"They, she has me attending these classes for domestic batterers, but I shouldn't even be attending these classes! I'm not like the other guys! We sit in a circle, and these guys talk about strangling their wives, throwing a radio at her in a tub of bath water! I've never done anything like that! I would never hurt Marti. I love her!"

"Well, did you ever do anything?"

"One time. Back in 1978. But it was just a misinterpretation. I would never hurt her! I love her!"

"What happened?"

"Well, she said she was going to leave me, and I freaked out, so I handed her a loaded gun — I wasn't going to hurt her — and I said, 'Go ahead! Shoot me! I can't live without you!"

We sat quietly together, staring at the wet, crumpled Kleenex tissue.

"I want her back! Can you get her back for me?"

"I can talk to her. I can tell her she won some free cosmetics. I can listen to what she has to say."

"Oh, I doubt she'd talk to you. She doesn't talk to strangers."

"You'd be surprised, Conrad," I confessed. "I have a way with people."

Conrad did not want me talking with Marti. Instead, he suggested I follow her to church and see what's up. She had recently joined a church and seemed to be spending an awful lot of time at nightly church functions. Conrad and I negotiated a plan. I'd see what's up at church and use it as a way to sell her some cosmetics.

At Choir Practice

There was a change in strategy. I decided to send my "son," to the church to see about becoming a church choir member.

After choir practice, my husband, I.J., took a paper from his shirt pocket and told everyone that his "mother," who sells cosmetics, was sponsoring a contest. The winner would receive $50 worth of free products. Several of the church members signed the sheet. Marti was one of them.

Eating hors d'oeuvres after the choir practice, Marti spoke at length to an older woman. As my husband eavesdropped on the conversation, he heard the two women talking endlessly in glowing terms about the woman's son, Tom.

Scrutinizing the Contest List

Back at my office, my husband and I carefully scrutinized the contest list. I.J. had the distinct impression that Marti was interested in Tom. But how could we determine Tom's address?

Checking the residential section of the telephone book, we discovered a Tom with the same last name as the older woman who had been talking with Marti and who had signed up for the cosmetic contest.

Watching Marti

The next day, I hired I.J. and my intern, Jim, to watch Marti at her parents' home. There was no action until two p.m. At that time, she entered her Mercedes and they followed her to Publix where she purchased two bags of groceries. She then stopped at a bank teller machine.

You Idiots!

A call came in from I.J. "We assumed she was going back home with the groceries. We lost her in traffic. We went back to her place, but her car is gone. What should we do now?"

"Meet me at Taco Bell," I told him.

"Yo Quiero Taco Bell"

Sipping on a Sprite, crunching on a bag of nachos, we came up with a plan. "Okay, I'm going to stake out her home," I told them. "Jim, you go to the church and see if she's there. I.J., you go see if she's at Tom's house."

I.J. protested. "You already sent me there the night we found his address. I doubt he's the boyfriend and I doubt she's there. Besides, it's clear across town. It'll be a waste of time. It's a bad plan and I don't want to go! Besides, she's got two bags of groceries with her. I say we stay staked out at her parents' house. She's got to show back up with the groceries before they spoil."

Working with a husband as a partner, you sometimes have conversations like this.

"Look, buddy," I told him. "You want the bed tonight — or the couch ?"

I.J. sighed resentfully. "I'm on my way to Tom's house," he grunted.

I Love Cops

Cops who park their cruisers at their home residence can be quite an asset to a private investigator. Rather than sitting in my tinted-window van out on a street, I'd much rather be sitting in someone's driveway. Cops make this possible.

Approaching the neat, little home with trimmed shrubs, two vehicles, a cruiser, and a boat in the driveway, I knocked on the door. A well-built young man wearing a tee shirt and a pair of gym shorts answered with a pleasant smile.

"Hi. My name is Angelina and I'm a private investigator." I flashed my I.D. and badge.

"Are you the police officer?" I inquired.

"I am," he said. "How can I help you?"

"I'm on a case right now. We're watching one of your neighbors. Would you mind if I sit in your driveway for a few hours?"

"Not at all," he replied. "In fact, you can sit inside here, if you want. It'll be more comfortable for you."

"Great!" The officer offered me some Gatorade. We spoke about crime, the new police chief, and police workshops that I conduct on *Police Communication in Traffic Stops* (my best-selling police book).

Soon, a call came in on my cell phone. It was I.J.

"You were right!" I.J. said. "She's here. She's having a cookout with Tom and some other guy!"

"I'll be right there!"

"Wait a second," I.J. declared. "There's really no place to park. He's the last house on the left on a dirt road next to a lake. There are barking dogs. You'll be discovered."

I called my partner, D.H. We agreed to meet in the parking lot at Food Lion and come up with a plan. Jim and I.J. were now off this case.

"It Looks Like a Nice Place to Live!"

D.H. and I decided to leave one car at the grocery store parking lot and drive one car down the dirt road. It was dusk. A woman at the first house when we turned onto Tom's street was exiting her driveway to take her dog for a walk. "Excuse me," I inquired from the passenger side of the car. "Are there any houses on this street for sale. It looks like such a nice place to live!"

"As a matter of fact, there is one," she replied. "The last house on the right is currently being renovated."

"Would you happen to know the owner's last name?"

"Yes, his name is Charles Chester."

"Oh! The former city commissioner?"

"Yes, I think so!"

"Oh! I think I'll give him a call and tell him to meet us here! Thank you so much!"

Perhaps we'll be your new neighbors," I told her.

"How 'bout a Meatball Sub Sandwich?"

D.H. and I drove his little car very slowly and unobtrusively down the little dirt road, backing into the carport, facing Tom's house. While D.H. videotaped the little threesome cookout party, I sat on the porch and eavesdropped on the conversation. Although I could not hear every word, I did overhear enough to get the drift of what was going on. There was lots of laughter. Tom's roommate is named Don. Both of them are divorced and also attend Marti's new church. Marti confessed that she was feeling a little drunk. As the sun set, and several hours had passed, Marti and Tom suggested getting meatball sub sandwiches for the three of them.

Marti moved her Mercedes, which was parked behind Tom's pick-up truck, nearer to the lake.

D.H. contacted me by walkie-talkie. "They're leaving. Should I follow them?"

"No," I said. "They're just going down to the deli to pick up meatball sub sandwiches. They'll be right back."

"Tell them to get me one!" D.H. chuckled. He had been sitting in a hot vehicle with the windows rolled up for about four hours. This is one of the "joys" of P.I. work.

Sure enough, the couple returned in about twenty minutes with the sub sandwiches. While the sun set, they ate their sandwiches. Marti swung in Tom's swing, and the three of them laughed and giggled and told one-liner jokes.

When the sun was completely down, the three of them moved into the house and turned on the television. I now moved into the car with D.H. We watched as they passed the kitchen window occasionally, getting drinks from the refrigerator, washing their hands, soaking the dishes, cleaning the counter. There was no evidence that Marti and Tom had reached a physical stage in their relationship.

Finally, at 10 p.m., Tom walked Marti to her Mercedes. We turned the video camera back on to night shot. Marti quickly entered her car and rolled down the window. A five-minute conversation ensued. Tom stood next to the driver window talking with Marti. After about five minutes, we saw his head duck down and, voila! — we captured the first kiss. Marti then started her vehicle, backed up, turned around, and drove away. Instead of immediately going back inside his house, Tom stood there in the dark, watching her vehicle as she drove off until he could see it no more. It was obvious by his body language that the man was lovesick for Marti. This was the beginning of a true romance.

"I Want Her Back!"

Conrad didn't want to watch the videotape. "Turn it off!" he whimpered. "I don't want to watch no more. I just want her back!"

"I don't think she's coming back any time soon, Conrad. I think she's in love."

"No, she'll be back," he said. "She did this to me once before — back in 1978. She came back."

"But it's not 1978 any more, Conrad."

Conrad was upset. "Well, then! Let's call the cops! Let's have her arrested! She's still a married woman!"

"What are we going to have her arrested for, Conrad?" I inquired. "For swinging on a swing? For eating a meatball sub sandwich!?"

"You don't understand," he said. "This is just like what happened to my mother and my father. She left my father and got involved with some guy who was in the Mafia. My father lost his business because of the Mafia. But then my mother got tired of her lover. My father took her back and they lived happily ever after in poverty. That's what's going to happen to me and Marti. It's the same."

I handed Conrad his videotape.

"Maybe I can hire you some more. Maybe you can go tell her she won the cosmetic contest. Then while you're talking to her, you can tell her I love her and I want her back."

I handed Conrad his receipt.

"You think about it, Conrad. I'll go talk to her, if that's what you want me to do, but I don't think she's coming back."

I heard no further from Conrad.

Call Pizza Girl for Your Next Portrait

A woman contacted my agency because she wanted to know to whom a phone number belonged. Checking the criss-cross Donnelly Directory, I was able to locate a name and an address that matched the phone number.

Now, my client had a second request. "This must be the woman my husband is seeing. I want a picture of her. Can you do that?"

"I can do better than that," I told her. "We'll get a video-tape of her."

This was a job for "pizza girl."

Clad in a full pizza delivery outfit (cap, name badge, shirt), I attached a magnetic pizza sign to the roof of my van and drove to her apartment. While I knocked on her front door, my husband hid inside the van, the eye of our video camera peeping through a small slit in the curtains.

"Yes?"

"Here's your pizza. The total is $9.27."

The woman looked confused. "I didn't order a pizza," she declared.

I carefully examined the order receipt. "Are you sure?"

"I'm positive," she retorted.

I rolled my eyes and made cutting remarks under my breath regarding my coworkers. "Would you happen to have a cell phone I could use?"

"I do, but feel free to come inside," she suggested. "You can use my regular phone."

"Oh, I'm not permitted inside a residence," I apologized.

When she returned with the cell phone, I made sure I was backed away from her front door far enough so that she would have to step out of her doorway. That way, I.J. could get a super shot. Then, I dialed my own office number, which rang and rang with no answer, obviously. (Now, I had her cell phone number on my caller ID.)

"The dipshits aren't even picking up the phone!" I declared. "Excuse my language."

"Sorry you're having such a bad day," she said, as I handed back her cell phone.

I.J. and I then drove back home and ate pizza for supper. Mission accomplished.

Mid-Life Crisis?

They say that when men turn forty, they suddenly get interested in sports cars, babes, and Grecian Formula 44. I think this was a classic case of this noted phenomenon. Instead of a sports car, however, Chester had recently purchased a brand new, top-of-the-line Harley-Davidson motorcycle.

His wife, Cindy, made an appointment to meet with me at my office. Upon entering she immediately handed me two small pieces of paper she had found in her husband's wallet. One piece read "Brandi" with a phone number on it. The other listed the name "Becky," also with a phone number on it. Prior to seeing me, she had confronted her husband. He said he had no idea how the phone numbers got into his wallet and that he had no clue who Becky and Brandi might even be. At first, she was going to just take his word at face value. But there were other strange events. Lately, her husband, Chester, had been spending a lot of time going off on his brand new, big black Harley-Davidson motorcycle. He had recently turned 40. He told his wife not to worry, that he simply drove off into the country or stopped at a local tavern just to have a few drinks and shoot the bull with some male acquaintances. The absent times were increasing in frequency and duration. Now, the wife wanted me to find out everything possible about Becky and Brandi. Who are these women? How does her husband know them?

The Strategy

My first strategy was to discover in what city the telephone numbers were located. They were not local exchanges, but no area codes had been written on the little scrap slips of paper. First, I discovered that both numbers are located in Jacksonville. Second, checking the criss-cross Donnelly Directory, I discovered that both numbers are unlisted.

The wife had told me the name of a restaurant/bar that her husband patronizes. So I called the bar and asked if they were hiring any waitresses. I wanted to know if Becky and Brandi might be waitresses at his favorite restaurant/bar. Through this phone call, I discovered that the establishment was a tavern located in Jacksonville and the patrons were working class people. There was no one named Brandi or Becky who was employed there.

Next, I decided to turn the phone numbers over to my partner, D.H.. He was instructed to call the women and play a guessing game with them in order to obtain as much information as possible. His script would go something like this:

Woman answers the phone. "Hello?"

My partner would then say, "Hey, baby! How you doin'? You remember me?"

She would then probably ask, "Who is this?" Or, she might say, "Hey. This is Gary. Right?" (At which point he would say "right" and then play along.)

The idea here is to play a guessing game and see how much information the caller can obtain. My partner might then ask, "Brandi, don't you remember giving me your phone number? I'd like to go out with you tonight, baby.

What are you doing tonight?" Eventually, he would ask her about work, her boyfriend(s), her address, etc.

When D.H. dialed Becky's number, however, he reached an answering machine. The message was short and curt and Becky did not sound particularly warm or friendly. "This is Becky. Leave a message at the tone." *(Click)*.

The second number was busy. When D.H. finally got through, a female answered, saying, "dressing room." He asked a few more questions and discovered that this was the dressing area for women who work at a ...*strip club!*

I then called the front business line and asked for Becky and Brandi. That's when I discovered that both Becky and Brandi are strippers who work the 7 p.m. 'til 2 a.m. shift.

Breaking the News

I contacted my client as soon as I discovered this disturbing news. Prior to dialing her number, I thought, "How will I tell her? What is the most diplomatic way of saying this?"

"Cindy," I said, "are you sitting down?"

"Yes."

"Are you alone?"

"Yes."

"Well, I'm trying to think of a nice way to put this." I paused.

"These women are 'professional' women — they are exotic dancers."

There was silence on the other end.

"Are you okay?" I finally asked.

"Yes. Yes. Don't tell me anymore. Let me think about this for a day or two," she said. "Right now, my heart is pounding out of my chest. I'll call you back in a couple of days."

A Week Later

Cindy called me back a week later to tell me the rest of the story.

Immediately after getting off of the phone with me, she had called her husband at their bar-b-cue restaurant. He answered the phone very jovially. "Good afternoon, this is Chester's Bar-b-cue Restaurant and Grill. How may I help you?"

She said to him in the sweetest tone, " Hi, Honey, can you hear me clearly?"

"Sure, sweetheart!" he replied. "What's up?"

She then pushed over his motorcycle. "Did you hear that sound, sweetheart?"

"Yes," he replied. "It sounded like something crashing."

"You're right," she said, pleasantly.

"What was that?"

"That was the sound of me pushing over your motorcycle."

There was silence on his end. Now, she took a can of spray paint and started to decorate the cycle. "And sweetheart, do you hear that?"

There was no reply.

"That's the sound of me spraying your motorcycle with bright yellow spray paint."

"I'll be right home," he replied.

Back at the House

Back at the house, the two of them had a long talk about the phone numbers she had found in his wallet.

"I don't know why I kept those numbers in my wallet," Chester confessed. "I went to that strip club with a couple of guys and those girls gave me their numbers. I never contacted either one of them and I meant to throw those numbers away," he explained.

That weekend, Chester planned an outing at the beach for his wife and kids. "I love you dearly," he told Cindy. "And I don't want to lose you. I promise I'll never do anything that stupid ever again."

A week had passed. The brand new Harley-Davidson still lay on its side in the garage with the bright yellow spray paint all over it.

Senior Citizen Romance

A 62-year-old man came into my office with a photo and two photocopies of letters he had just found in his 59-year-old wife's brief case. "I just found this stuff when I was snooping in my wife's portfolio," he stated. "Claudia is an art instructor, and lately, she has been spending a lot of time away from home. What do you think of these letters?" he inquired.

The first letter was a journal that contained some really lame poetry. A man was documenting the giddy love feelings he was experiencing during a week after meeting my client's wife. He said he was fantasizing all weekend, while babysitting his screaming grandchildren, about being with her, holding her, kissing her. As a married man, he said he felt simultaneously elated and guilty that he was experiencing these giddy feelings that had remained dormant for so many decades in his soul.

At one point in the letter, he included colorful children's stickers of cartoon characters and wrote gushy messages beside each sticker. "Why am I writing these things?" he wrote. "I feel like a love-sick teenager all over again."

The second letter was a reply from my client's wife. In the letter, she indicated that she, too, had been experiencing giddy feelings of elation. "But," she added, "I love my husband and even though we have had no sexual contact in five years, I do not wish to divorce him." She did suggest, however, that she and the man meet for coffee after art classes. The letter contained a postscript. "I also own a condo at the beach where we can simply 'hang out' as platonic best friends."

The husband wanted me to discover the name, phone number, address, and everything else possible regarding the man who was standing with his arm around his wife in the photo.

Tapping Claudia's E-Mail

The first thing that George wanted me to do was to find a way to tap into his wife's e-mail account. This would tell us how far the relationship had progressed since the letters had been written and what plans the lusty geriatrics had made behind George's back. Since the e-mail account was in George's name, it was perfectly legal for us to tap into her e-mail writings.

I hired a team of computer experts who agreed to meet with me at George's house when his wife was away at a doctor's appointment. The four of us posed as a home cleaning service agency, in case his wife should suddenly surprise us with an unexpected visit. While the two men worked on having all of Claudia's e-mail messages forwarded to their computer, their female partner guarded the side door and George and I toured the house, pretending to be taking notes regarding the cleaning particulars of each room.

One Week Later

A week had passed and there had been no e-mail correspondence between Claudia and the man.

"That seems very odd," I told my client. "Did you let Claudia know in any way that she was being investigated?"

"Not really," George replied. "But I did turn on our home video camera and leave it running on the counter where it could capture anything going on on her computer screen. Then I left for the day."

Naturally, when George returned home, the video camera had been turned off. There was nothing recorded on the videotape. I felt slightly piqued at George. This is a common occurrence in the P.I. business. Someone hires a private investigator. Then they become too involved in the case themself. In the process, they botch the case and thereby make it more difficult to get anything accomplished. "George, you should not have left a video camera running on the counter," I mildly scolded him.

"Yes, I realize that now. She went out and got her own P.O. box the next day. I think they're now corresponding by mail only."

Next, George wanted me to follow her on Saturday. He was certain that she would be driving somewhere to meet the man. I told him that I was not available on Saturday — that I had already contracted with another client but that I could follow her on Sunday or the following week.

George was upset. "Well! I'll just have to hire someone else!" he spouted.

I suggested that he give it a little time, since the wife would now be extra cautious after having discovered the video camera. But George was antsy. He wanted to find something out immediately.

Conclusion

George did hire one of my competitors to watch his wife for the next two days. During that time, the investigator did not see Claudia with the man.

After paying for two days' of investigation, George became impatient. He confronted his wife with the photocopies of the letters and the photos and demanded an explanation. Claudia broke down and cried and admitted that she had felt attracted to the man. She did promise George that she would stop seeing the man and that no sexual contact had ever taken place.

The geriatric romance had been aborted.

Chapter Four
Fruitcakes!

At least once a week, a total nutcase is going to call you for P.I. services if you are listed in the Yellow Pages. Many P.I.s blow off these kinds of calls, but even paranoid schizophrenics, manic depressives, and major depressives can provide a good source of income and amusement. Here are a few guidelines up front:

1. **Take them seriously.** First of all, you don't know, at the start, if they might not have a legitimate point. Listen carefully. Take notes. There might be some validity in what they are telling you.

2. **By listening and empathizing, the fruitcake may be getting something off his chest.** You may be instrumental in bringing that person back down to some level of reality. What you investigate for them, no matter how ludicrous their claim, may be something they need to hear and discover. If they have come to trust you, you may be helpful in getting them zoned back down to Planet Earth.

The Government is in My Attic

Early on a Thursday morning, I received a call on my business line from an elderly lady.

"I'm here at the mall," she began, in whispered tones. "I can't talk for too long by phone because they'll see me. Can you meet with me somewhere as soon as possible?"

I was curious to know the problem, but I bit my tongue. "I'll meet you in twenty minutes at the Holiday Inn next to the mall."

Twenty minutes later, we were upstairs in the conference building, alone in a cozy, living-room setting. Mrs. White leaned forward while she sat on the corner of the sofa. I was to her right in an adjacent chair, ready to jot notes on her every word.

"You're not going to believe this," she started, looking as though she was about to burst into tears, "but the government has been following me, watching me, harassing me every minute of every waking day for the past nine years."

I didn't know what to tell her. For a start, I assumed that what she was telling me might be true. How do I know? Perhaps the government has time to watch her, but I was curious to know why. By appearance, she seemed quite normal. An elderly lady, very well dressed, wearing a two piece suit, Jacqueline Kennedy style, a pill box hat on her head, neat little pearls around her neck, a tiny purse with a gold clip clasp in the middle of her lap. She placed the purse on the corner of the coffee table in front of her, smoothed out her skirt, and continued.

"I know it sounds odd, but you've got to believe me."

"I believe you," I said, "but why are they bothering you?"

"I've wondered that myself," she stated, "and I think I finally figured it out. Nine years ago, I got what appeared to be an innocent-looking letter in the mail. It was a form letter from the U.S. Treasury Department asking me if I was interested in purchasing U.S. Savings Bonds. Well, I wrote them back and told them, 'No, thank you. I already have purchased some savings bonds. I heard about them through my friend, John Brown.'"

"I see."

"For years, it didn't bother me that they were watching my every move, but lately, they have been up in my attic pouring an invisible gas on me when I'm trying to sleep, and it's just awful, just awful! I've had to move into the living room to try and catch some sleep. But, last week, it was the final straw. They moved above me in the living room and have been pouring more invisible gas on me!"

"But, why are they doing this?"

"I finally figured it out. When I wrote them about the U.S. Savings Bonds, apparently, they wanted my friend, John Brown, very badly. What they don't know is that he died back in 1984. But they are continuing to look for him and they think he's going to show up at my house."

"Why don't you call them and tell them that he's dead?"

"I did. I called the U.S. Treasury in North Carolina, where they first contacted me, and I tried to explain that they don't need to bother me any more, that he is dead, but they pretended that they didn't know what I was talking about. They're very clever, you know."

"Everything they have done to me reminds me exactly of what they did to those poor people in Waco, Texas. It's the same thing all over again. And once you catch them, I want to sue them for one million dollars for every year that they have been harassing me. And then you and I can split the money!"

"I see." I glanced out the window at the pool, tapped my foot, then responded. "But, you know, the government is very clever. I don't know if I'll ever really be able to catch them," I confessed.

She leaned toward me.

"Here's what I can do, however. I can go up there in the attic and sprinkle a special poison that only affects the government," I said.

"It won't hurt me?"

"No. It won't hurt you. And then, I will harass them so bad that they will be so sorry that they ever contacted you in the first place. I'll guarantee you that they will never bother you again."

"Oh, bless your heart!" she said, bursting into tears and squeezing my hands. "I knew when I checked the Yellow Pages this morning at the mall that Jesus would lead me to the right ad!"

"Yes, indeed," I assured her.

She opened her purse and blew her nose with a little hankie. Recomposing herself, she said, "But I'm afraid that as soon as you go up there, they'll know, and then they'll go away."

I thought about that for a moment. "You know. You've got a point. Hold on," I told her. "Let me call my husband. I think this is going to be a two-person job."

My red-headed husband arrived in about 15 minutes and Mrs. White took an instant liking to him. I said, "I'm going to leave the two of you alone now. I have another job to do. I'll call you later, Mrs. White, and figure out what the two of you have decided."

Later that day, I learned the strategy that my husband and Mrs. White had come up with.

Like many clients, Mrs. White was a wanna-be P.I. By getting her involved in the process, she was more than willing to pay for our services.

Mrs. White determined that the only way we could catch the government in her attic would be if I.J. dressed up as her in her night clothes, drove her car up to her condo, parked it, walked in, and then slept in Mrs. White's bed, posing as her. When he would feel the "gas" released into the room, he would charge up into the attic and catch them. The plan was set.

Mrs. White never called back to initiate the plan. Maybe the government in the attic accomplished *their* plan?

My Husband is Trying to Kill Me

She met with me at our scheduled time in the lobby at the Holiday Inn accompanied by her husband. He handed her $500 in cash and I told the two of them to follow me to the conference room where there are living-room settings, so we could have more privacy.

"Oh, no. He's not joining us," my client said. Then she ordered her husband to pick her up in approximately two hours.

While we sat adjacent to one another in a plush chair and sofa, Anna began a somewhat scattered story. She hadn't seen her children since they were very little. They had been taken away from her by HRS and given to their blood father. Where are they? How are they doing? She said she wanted to know everything possible about them. But, could her husband possibly be listening in right now? She didn't want him to hear what she was about to tell me. We looked around and I told her no one seemed to be in sight, but Anna was not convinced. He probably was lurking somewhere in a hallway listening to our conversation. I checked the hallway and reported back to her that I could not find/see her husband anywhere. She said she knew he had fathered the children of a woman in Jacksonville and how could I get a hold of their birth certificates to prove he had had an affair? And also, did I know that she is kin to Rose Kennedy? I said I had no idea. She then informed me that Rose Kennedy assumed the pseudonym of Virginia Woolf and died at 102 in St. Augustine, where she had secretly lived for many years. Anna wanted me to check and see if something was left for her in Mrs. Kennedy's will. She was certain that something would turn up. Which brought her back to the matter of her husband. They had gone to Nations Bank earlier that day and obtained a $1,000 loan in order to get the money to pay me. She was certain that her husband and the bank loan officer had secretly collaborated to have her sign a life insurance policy because her husband was planning to kill her to get the money. She also wanted me to check with the Global Life Insurance company and find out how many life insurance policies were in her name. Apparently, there were other people who might want her dead, also, so they could collect on her. She asked me if I believed in Jesus, and then we prayed together. Taking a napkin from her purse, she wrote a brief note on it that she wanted me to notarize. It read, "If I should die, my children are the sole heirs to everything I own."

"If you don't hear back from me by tomorrow, will you call the police?"

"Of course I will," I assured her. "But if you feel you're in that much danger, why don't you stay at the women's shelter or a hotel?"

"Because it doesn't really matter," she said. "You're going to take care of everything I need." There was a beat of silence and she looked outside at the pool.

Turning back to me, she said, "Why did you ask me that? Do you **really** think I'm in danger?"

"Well, I don't know. Why do you think your husband wants to kill you?"

"I didn't say he **wants** to kill me!" she replied, defensively. "I said he might **try** to kill me!" she explained. "There's a big difference, you know!"

"I see." I tapped my pen on my notepad. "So, how long have you been with your husband?"

"Which one?"

"The one you're with now."

"Twelve years."

"That's a long time. Has he ever tried to hurt you before?"

"No. But I know he's tried. My first husband tried, too."

"Well, why don't we call the police and report him?"

Anna became extremely agitated with me. She stood up and pounded her right fist into her left palm. "Because they'll put me in a straight jacket and take me away! Don't you get it!? Don't you understand anything!!? They'll believe him! And I'm not going back to the nut house! There is **nothing** wrong with me!"

"I see."

"Don't you believe me!?"

"Of course I believe you."

"And you've been saved."

"Yes. I've been saved."

She calmed down a bit and resumed her seat on the sofa.

"I know a lot of things," she told me. "I know things that no one else knows."

"I believe you."

"I'll tell you something if you promise not to tell anyone."

"I promise."

She leaned forward and lowered her voice. "John Kennedy, Jr., his wife, and sister-in-law are all still alive."

"Really!"

"Yes. They parachuted into the water and were rescued. Mrs. Kennedy is pregnant with a boy child and they didn't want him to have to live with all the media publicity, so they staged their deaths and now they're living on a secluded island."

"Very interesting."

"You believe me, don't you?"

"Yes. Of course I believe you."

"And you've been saved."

"Yes. I've been saved."

"Then let's pray some more. You say the prayers this time."

We held hands, bowed our heads and prayed for Anna's safety. We prayed that God would guide me in finding her children. We prayed that Anna would find peace. She cried. My eyes grew a little moist. We stood up and she embraced me.

"And remember," she said. "If you don't hear from me again, give my love to my two children, Jonathan and Lisa."

"I promise I will."

I began the investigation immediately, which I completed in about six hours. I called her the next day to tell her I was successful at locating her son, who spoke to me at length and told me everything about him and his sister. I had also obtained all the other information she had sought, or at least found ways for her to obtain the additional information herself. But when I called her home phone number, her husband said she was "out" and he didn't know when she would be returning. He promised he'd have her call me upon her arrival.

Three days passed and I heard no word from Anna. I called her number repeatedly, but there was never any answer. Finally, around 11:30 p.m. on the third day, I contacted the local sheriff's department and reported her as a missing person. I said, "I don't know if I'm doing the right thing, but she told me she thought her husband was about to kill her. She paid me a large sum of money in cash and she didn't want a receipt. It's been three days. I have called her home phone repeatedly and obtained no answer except for the first call, so I am a bit alarmed." The sheriff's department assured me that I was doing the right thing. They promised they'd ring me in a few hours.

I waited up and around 1 a.m., the sheriff's department called back. Two sheriffs had reported to the scene. The trailer was completely dark. They knocked for about twenty minutes and then announced that they were about to break down the door. At that time, a very agitated looking Anna opened the door and asked what they wanted. They told her I was concerned and had reported her missing. She assured them she would contact me in the morning. Then the officer told me, "By the way, Anna's record is flagged. She calls us at least once a week to report that her husband is about to kill her. She's been claiming her husband is about to murder her for many years."

Another three days passed and I heard no word from Anna. Finally, I mailed the report to her with a green card, requiring her signature, along with a refund check of $250. Two days passed. When I returned home from another assignment, I checked my answering machine. And there was a brief, hostile-sounding message from Anna. The message said, "I got your check."

There was a long pause. And then in a very snide-sounding tone, she continued. "And, today, I'm **thinking** of cashing it." And she slammed down the receiver.

Anna did, in fact, cash the check. The report I wrote for her appears below.

(By the way, I never heard from her ever again. I hope the report brought her some kind of peace of mind.)

Angela V. Woodhull, Ph.D.
P.O. Box 14423
Gainesville, FL 32604
(352) 332-7746

Date: XXXXX
RE: INFORMATION YOU REQUESTED

You contacted my Agency, AAAAA Investigative Services, on XXXXX. We met at the Holiday Inn XXXXX on this same date and you hired me at my 10 hour rate of $50.00 per hour to do a variety of things:

1. Contact your son, XXXXX, D.O.B. XXXXX and see how he is doing and what is going on in his life.

2. Find out where your daughter, XXXXX attends college and what is going on in her life.

3. Talk in person with XXXXX at Nations Bank regarding the $1,000 loan you received on XXXXX and determine if there is life insurance on this loan.

4. Contact Globe Life Insurance and discover if there are any life insurance policies in your name.

5. Find out if you are in the will of Virginia Woolf or Wolf who died in St. Augustine in either 1997 or 1998 at the age of 102.

Here are the results of my investigations and inquiries.

1. CONTACT WITH XXXXX

Beginning at approximately 6 p.m. on XXXXX 1999, I dialed the number for XXXXX in XXXXX Michigan where XXXXX resides.

From approximately 6 p.m. until 9 p.m., there was no answer. I tried the call approximately once every 10 minutes.

Beginning around 9 p.m., I received a busy signal. The line stayed busy until almost around midnight. I did call again at that time, since it was only 11 p.m., Michigan time, and Mr. XXXXX did answer the phone, saying he had been on the Internet for several hours talking with his friends and the last hour, he had been e-mailing/talking with his sister; hence, the busy signal. XXXXX is doing very well. He is doing well in school and he plans on going to college on a football scholarship. He would like to attend either Grand Valley or Western. He would like to major in possibly physical therapy or athletic assistance or sports therapy. He has not yet completely decided. All last year, he had a steady girlfriend, but she broke up with him recently. However, he took another girl named XXXXX to the homecoming dance two weeks ago and the possibility of a steady relationship with her looks promising. In fact, on October 20, they plan on celebrating their one-month anniversary. They will hang out together and rent movie videos for their celebration. XXXXX is a beautiful girl who has blonde highlights in her hair. She runs cross-country and is on the track team of her high school. When talking with his sister, by e-mail prior to receiving a call from me, he and his sister were noting how terrific life was going for each of them. Both are extremely pleased and happy with their lives.

2. XXXXX is attending college at XXXXX State University. She is majoring in political science. She wrote an essay last year, which won her a ton of money for college. She is receiving really good grades and she is going with XXXXX — they have been going steady for the past 2½ years. XXXXX attends college at XXXXX Tech.

XXXXX and XXXXX were just discussing their biological parents by e-mail. XXXXX said he plans on contacting both of his biological parents on his 18th birthday — April 23rd, 2000. He is scared, but everyday he thinks about doing this and he is growing in confidence. He lifts weights everyday. Everyday, while he lifts weights, he thinks about his biological mom and dad and what he's going to say on April 23 when he has the confidence to pick up the phone and dial them and speak with them. Last year, he said his biological mother did contact him but he was so startled and surprised by this — it threw him off balance, and he didn't know how to handle it or what to say, so he just hung up the phone. He is sorry that he did this, but even if his biological mother contacted him again right now, he would probably do the same thing because he is *not totally ready* to speak with her as yet, but he does promise to call on his birthday or sometime shortly thereafter. XXXXX is taking the lead from her brother. She also wants to contact her biological parents when XXXXX does or shortly thereafter. They want both of their biological parents to be proud of them, know that they are okay, and know that they are doing great in life. They feel no ill will toward either of their biological parents.

Power lifting gives XXXXX confidence and motivation. XXXXX is living in the dorms. XXXXX did not have her mailing address or phone number, since they have been exclusively corresponding frequently by e-mail. He will get it for me, if I contact him again. His live-in parents are also doing fine and he is happy with his relationship with them. He feels close to his sister.

3. XXXXX at Nation's Bank showed me the papers in her trashcan, which are getting ready to go into the shredder. She provided me with a brief note on a pink piece of paper, which is attached to the report. The first loan, which included loan payback protection (i.e., life insurance), was torn in half very dramatically in front of XXXXX and is being disposed of. A new and second loan application was filled out and many new papers had to be signed all over again. This time, the $1,000 loan was guaranteed with a bank CD. There is no life insurance whatsoever on the second new loan.

4. There are six Globe Insurance companies listed on the Internet: Arizona — (602) 277-6779; Kentucky — (606) 356-8773; Ohio — (513) 871-3330; Kentucky — (606) 727-2226; California — (813) 783-5585, Oklahoma City, Oklahoma — (405) 270-1410. The first five offices said there are NO life insurance policies written on XXXXX, DOB XXXXX. The sixth company, located in Oklahoma City, said there were LAPSED POLICIES for XXXXX but NOT a XXXXX born 1-8-56. These LAPSED POLICIES are for a

XXXXX(s) who lived(s) in Clearwater, St. Petersburg, Baywood, Hudson, and New Port Ritchie, Florida. NONE of these XXXXX possess the birthdate of XXXXX. ALL POLICIES are LAPSED.

There is also an insurance hot line for the state of Florida: 1-800-342-2762. To find out if an insurance policy has been taken out on an individual, one must contact EACH and EVERY INSURANCE company listed in the United States. For example, under Global Insurance, there are 22 listings alone in the United States. Each and every one of the 22 listings would have to be individually contacted. This service can be provided for you, if you so desire.

5. HOW TO OBTAIN A DEATH CERTIFICATE FOR VIRGINIA WOOLF(E). The information line (recorded message) in Tallahassee, provided me with the following information:

Provide their office with the full legal name of the deceased person, the county, state, and date of death. If searching by years (i.e., you don't have the specific date), include $2 extra for each year searched. Tell what relationship you are to the deceased and why you want the information and why you have an interest in their estate. The fee is $5 for the first certified death certificate and $4 for each additional copy. The money is non-refundable, even if no death certificate is located. If you pay $15, they will rush the order to you within 3 working business days. If you wish to pay by credit card, you can, but there is an additional $4.50 charge for using a credit card. They accept only four credit cards: Visa, MasterCard, American Express, or Discover. If you send a money order, mail payment and the above information to: Office of Vital Statistics, PO Box 210, Jacksonville, FL 32231-0042. For ordering by credit card, dial (904) 359-6911.

You also asked if I could find out who the blood father is for the five children of XXXXX. There is one XXXXX listed for Jacksonville, Florida, if you would like me to try to contact her and speak directly with her. According to the birth certificate record center in Jacksonville, I would have to see the birth certificates directly from the mother in order to get that information. But, according to Sharon Nixon, who works birth certificate records, oftentimes, the blood father's name is not even listed on the birth certificate, if he does not sign the back of the birth certificate form.

This concludes the investigation that you specified. I am charging you for five hours of my time, plus long distance, and travel. Time was spent in contacting agencies, your son, and two meetings with you.* At the $50 rate, your bill is $250. This leaves a credit of $250, which can be either refunded to you or used for additional services.

END OF REPORT

* and report writing, approximately one hour.

ADDENDUM

I am also available for talking with your husband regarding the mysterious phone calls that are being made on a regular basis to your home. Please let me know if you would like the three of us to have a discussion. I would first talk with your husband alone and then draw you into the conversation.

Also, I did not generate the two $100 each reports on XXXXX and XXXXX since the phone conversation with XXXXX seemed to produce the information you desired. However, I can still run those reports for $200, if you desire.

It was a pleasure meeting you and doing business with you. You will remain in my prayers.

Angela Woodhull

Chapter Five
Busted!

Every year, thousands of people fake injuries on the job in an attempt to milk millions of dollars out of their former employers. While some people feel sorry for the folks who are exaggerating their injuries, many sympathize with the employer who must pay exorbitant amounts to workers who are generally not even hurt. Contact insurance companies and let them know you will do your first job at a greatly reduced rate, just to get your foot in the door. When you get a "yes," keep in mind the following points.

1. **Insurance companies are looking for lots of good video footage.** They want to see the subject walking, turning, moving, bending, and perhaps, lifting objects.

2. **If the subject leaves his or her home, continue to videotape the premises.** By showing on video that the subject remained away from home for several hours, the claim adjusters will be able to demonstrate that the subject is not as disabled as he or she is claiming.

3. **If the subject does leave the premises, it is good to have two vehicles on the scene.** While one car follows the subject's car, the other vehicle follows the P.I.'s car. Then, leap frog, so that the subject is less likely to discover that he or she is being followed. Use walkie-talkies to keep in touch.

4. **Here are a few more techniques that can be used to capture a subject out in his or her yard:**

   a. **Pretend that you and your partners are "land surveyors."** Purchase magnetic signs for your van and fake I.D.s, in case you are questioned. While two people pretend to be conducting actual land surveying work, one is inside the van videotaping.

   b. **Likewise, you can also pretend that you are engineers.** Have magnetic signs and fake I.D.s. Use the same procedures as above.

   c. **You can also set up a time-lapse camera in the area and let it videotape the subject's premises for one week.**

   d. **Canvas the neighborhood as a cosmetic salesperson or as a real estate investor.** One of the techniques you can use is going inside a neighbor's house. Once inside, you can safely videotape from their bathroom window (assuming a window is available), keeping the operation covert.

   e. **Pose as a pizza delivery person.** Contact the subject and tell him you just got two wrong orders and if he wants one of the two pizzas, come on out to your van and take a look (you're too lazy to actually deliver the free pizza to his door). If he comes out and takes the one free pizza, wait until he's back inside with it, then go back up to his door and tell him he can go get the other free pizza. Of course, while he's making these trips out to your car, he's being videotaped, now, isn't he?

f. **What if the subject wakes up one morning and discovers that there's a bunch of trash strewn all over his front yard?** Of course, he'll be motivated to clean it up, and you'll just happen to be watching, videotaping.

g. **If the neighborhood is right, you might want to set up a tent.** Capture your subject on videotape from inside your tent.

h. **Or, you can be sunbathing across the way in your lawn chair, reading a book.** For this type of surveillance, you'll want to purchase the smallest video camera, shaped like a small 5" x 5" book. Now, cut a hole through the binding of the book, and set the camera inside. It will look like you're reading a Stephen King novel on a hot, summer day.

Over the Fence

Sometimes you'll get calls from the big boys — you know — the big P.I. firms that want to farm out their jobs to the little guys. These jobs can be both fun and rewarding, or frustrating and nerve-wracking, depending on whom you're working for. The following is a description of a workman's comp case I was hired to do for a large south-Florida-based P.I. firm. When the owner of the firm contacted me, he said that he had already hired another P.I. to conduct surveillance on the subject with little success. Now, he was willing to try out my agency and he wanted to know what I would charge him for two days of surveillance, eight hours per day. Having no idea, I asked him what was the going rate. When he told me it was $20 to $25 per hour, I scoffed and counter-offered with $35 per hour plus $.31 per mile. He faxed me a copy of the agreement and the next day, my intern and I were on our way.

This was my first workman's comp case, so I didn't really know what to expect. A friend of mine, who used to be a P.I. in Maryland, said that it wouldn't be as difficult as I would expect. "People who fake disabilities are usually pretty stupid and pretty easy to catch," he said. His prediction turned out to be accurate, but at first, this wasn't really the case.

What made this job difficult right from the start was the layout of the neighborhood. It turned out that the subject, Mr. Allen, lived in a small, close-knit community on a lake. At best, you could describe this neighborhood as "Dog Patch," where residents used chicken wire for fences that encompassed grassless yards with lots of large, barking dogs. It was the kind of neighborhood where all the men drive large pick up trucks, and when a strange vehicle enters the community, everyone takes notice within a few minutes. The neighbors all socialize with one another and phone one another if an odd vehicle is parked anywhere on one of their sugar sand roads.

My partner and I drove around the neighborhood for a good twenty minutes very early on a Saturday morning before anyone was up and about. Only the dogs and the roosters took notice of us. After circling the dirt roads several times, we finally decided to park right inside the yard of a neat little cottage home two blocks south of our subject. Although we'd need binoculars to observe Mr. Allen if he should exit his trailer, we felt certain that he would not suspect that we were P.I.s. In fact, we unloaded our bicycles and took turns riding around the neighborhood.

Somewhere around 11 a.m., Mr. Allen stepped outside and our filming began. Later I wrote a detailed report, which described our investigative methods and techniques:

RE: Mr. Allen

The following is a detailed description of a two-day investigation regarding Mr. Allen who allegedly is suffering from a disabling condition of back and neck pain. Mr. Allen is a 47-year-old white male with gray hair about seven inches long. He is approximately 5' 10" and weighs approximately 155 lbs.

To prepare for this investigation, my partner, private investigator intern D.H. and I packed up a white Chevy van with walkie-talkies, video camera, three changes of outfits, including various hats and sunglasses, two pairs of binoculars, two bicycles, roller blades, and a door-to-door cosmetic sales kit.

FIRST DAY: Leaving Gainesville at 7 a.m., I picked up my partner. We arrived in Springtown, Florida at 10 a.m. Computer directions to find Mr. Allen's residence were not completely accurate. It took one additional hour of driving up and down County Road 11 and checking with clerks at the local convenience store and the post office (who had no knowledge of how to find 48th Avenue). Using trial and error, we finally headed south on 88th Street and, at last, located Mr. Allen's residence, which is located in a small village adjacent to a lake. (The computer directions indicated we should turn on 48th Avenue, which did not exist, we finally concluded.)

We circled the area and finally decided to set up surveillance operations in the front yard of Shirley and Paul Lowman (as the welcome sign indicated near their driveway entrance). The Lowmans were obviously not at home, so we figured that if anyone approached us, we would simply say we were old friends visiting from Ohio, coming to surprise the Lowmans. Although no one approached us, several residents did take notice of our presence. Beginning at approximately 10 a.m., D.H. videotaped Mr. Allen's residence for about 10 seconds, every half hour.

At approximately 11 a.m., Mr. Allen was seen exiting his front door. At that time, I rode my bicycle to his next door neighbor's house and struck up a conversation with one of the men in the yard, a semi-toothless male. I said I was inquiring about the For Sale sign and wanted to know the selling price. He said that the property is not really for sale. Instead, it is for rent but the owner couldn't find a For Rent sign so he put up the For Sale sign and that it's actually the trailer next door that is for rent, $60 per week and that includes all utilities, including a working phone. While we talked, I noticed Mr. Allen walking from his front yard to the side of his house where he unlatched the hood of a light brown colored vehicle and appeared to be checking the oil. He then closed the hood, started the vehicle, drove around to the front of his house, where his wife, carrying what appeared to be a bank bag, entered the vehicle and off they drove. (11:06 a.m.)

Around 2 p.m., the Lowmans pulled up into their driveway. They had already been forewarned by some of their neighbors that we were in their yard. I exited my van and greeted them graciously, telling them that I was extremely happy to see them and I thanked them for allowing us to use their yard to conduct surveillance on the unwanted drug dealers who were invading their neighborhood and hadn't they already been contacted regarding our arrival? There must have been some misunderstanding. We showed our I.D.s and, as usual, my "sales job" worked. The Lowmans were delighted to be "part" of some big undercover drug investigation. We used their bathrooms, were given a grand tour of their cottage, and Mrs. Lowman showed me her craft room. I oohed and aahed over the crafts and promised to buy a gift basket the next day (which I indeed did). Shirley Lowman said that tomorrow was her birthday, so we also returned the next day with a birthday cake, some ice cream, 58 candles, nonalcoholic champagne, and a small gift (a jewelry music box).

Paul Lowman and D.H. watched the Gator game from the television inside the craft room. It was from this angle that. D.H. was able to spot Mr. Allen return home with his wife at approximately 3 p.m. Mr. Allen proceeded to work on his other vehicle, a truck, for several hours. At this point, D.H. and I drove our bicycles to the lake and parked our bicycles in a T position and pretended to be carrying on a conversation. While I looked at the lake, D.H. peered over my shoulder and videotaped Mr. Allen picking up various tools and repairing his truck. At approximately 4 p.m., a friend of

Mr. Allen's arrived to assist in the vehicle repair. On videotape, you'll see a good seven minutes where Mr. Allen is underneath the truck with his head up, holding a light. At 4:59 p.m. his wife gives him a hand up off the ground. Later, however, he's back under the truck and gets up without assistance (6:05 p.m.).

SECOND DAY: We left Gainesville at 11 a.m. and arrived in Springtown at 12:30 p.m. Mr. Allen did not leave his residence at all during the time we conducted our investigation. The Lowmans informed us that Mr. Allen's father, who lives on the street behind the Lowmans, observed D.H. videotaping his son underneath his truck for several minutes and he wanted to know what that was all about. The Lowmans said that we were videotaping the entire area, looking to buy property. With our new pretext in place, we spent the next two hours interviewing neighbors, explaining that an investor is interested in buying the entire village and building condos for tourists. What would be their selling prices?, we inquired.

Eventually, we arrived at the house next door to Mr. Allen's. On this day, we spoke directly to Mr. Allen's landlord and landlady, Roy and Annie (the ones with the For Sale sign that means "For Rent"). Annie provided me with a tour of her home. Roy offered to take a look at my van to see what was causing the "whining" sound. After touring her home and the $60 a week trailer, we drove the van from the Lowmans' yard over to Roy's, where three men looked under the hood and then added power steering fluid to my van, which did, indeed, fix the whiny noise. Now, it was raining, so we stayed under the carport and talked with Roy, a very large man, very friendly, who said he himself is in very poor health. He took a letter out of his back pocket which verified his poor health, a letter from a doctor in Ocala, dated 1997, announcing that Roy has less than a year to live due to congestive heart failure, and that he cannot be operated on because he also has high blood pressure, kidney and liver failure, and sugar diabetes. Despite it all, he appears to be high-spirited and says he just takes one day at a time. He then told us a couple of jokes. He said, "I am the nibby nose of the neighborhood, so if you want to know anything about this place or anybody in it, just ask me." His wife said she would give us a tour of the house next door, where Mr. Allen and his wife reside, but not until after Mr. and Mrs. Allen's company departed. Of the Allens, Roy told us the following: Mr. and Mrs. Allen are loners with few friends. They do not socialize with any of the neighbors, including their next door neighbors, landlords, Roy and Annie. Both Mr. and Mrs. Allen are retired military. Approximately one year ago, Mr. Allen told them he fell off a tractor trailer rig when he was putting on the tarp. Roy said he continually complains that he suffers from back and neck problems, "But I just don't see it," said Roy. "He's always out there working on his vehicles or going off fishing. Looks like he has the life of Riley to me." Roy said that Mr. Allen has trained his wife to do all the yard work, that Mrs. Allen has been trained by Mr. Allen to be a very hard working woman, while he has fun playing. "Who knows, maybe he is injured. He sure complains enough, but it don't look that way to me." He said Mr. Allen also stays inside a lot, playing on his computer. When he had his injury, his wife went to school and learned how to drive a big truck. She now goes to work, operating a dump truck. He was under the impression that Mr. Allen receives a pension from the military and is currently applying for workman's comp due to his injury of one year ago. The Allens pay Roy and Annie $75 per week in rent and they are always on time. The property has orange, lemon, lime, and tangerine trees on it. If my "husband" D.H. and I wish to stay in the trailer for one week, we can do so for $60.

It began raining, so we decided to leave early to give us the extra one and a half hours for report writing and tape duplication. Mr. Allen was still inside his house with his wife and vehicle-repair-helping friend.

END OF REPORT

When my partner and I left early on Sunday, we were delighted with the results. It was a "slam dunk" — at least in our opinion. I couldn't wait to call my client, Mr. Weinberg, and tell him about our success. We hurried and faxed him the report and Federal Expressed the videotape, which depicted not only our footage of Mr. Allen but also various aspects of the adventure (such as buying the ice cream, interacting with the landlord, filming other people's yards and homes). Our client was livid. He screamed, ranted, and raved and said he would be the laughing stock of the P.I. business if he sent such a tape to the insurance company. He asked for my agency license number and threatened to turn me in to the state of Florida for incompetence. He complained that our pictures were too shaky and too far away. He raged that we did not follow Mr. Allen when he left his premises. I tried to explain in between his bursts of shouting that Mr. Allen would certainly have known we were following him and so we decided to stay put. In actuality, we had done a superb job. Because we did not follow Mr. Allen, he felt certain he was not being observed by us, and, hence, he spent four hours repairing vehicles (which was much better evidence than videotaping him pushing a supermarket cart, making a bank deposit, picking up his mail, or eating lunch with his wife at a restaurant). Our client, Mr. Weinberg, said he would not be paying us because we were tacky, bumbling morons.

The next day, I contacted an attorney friend, Mr. Philstein, and described what happened. Being fully familiar with my work, since he has used me on a number of occasions, my attorney bud said that big-city south Florida investigators have a reputation for being a bit on the unscrupulous side. "If you got the guy on video working on and underneath a van, that sounds pretty damn good," he said. He offered to contact Mr. Weinberg on my behalf and make sure I received payment for services rendered.

A few days later, while in the middle of preparing a chronological report for Attorney Philstein so he could properly confront Mr. Weinberg, I received a call from the non-paying Mr. Weinberg. Now, suddenly, Mr. Weinberg was saying that the videotape I had sent him was really not so bad after all, but that additional footage was needed by the insurance company. He asked me how much I would charge him to stay in the $60 a week trailer and videotape Mr. Allen as much as possible. I was flabbergasted. I told him I'd "think about it" and get back with him.

I called my attorney bud, Mr. Philstein, and said, "Guess what. He's changed his mind about my being incompetent. Now he wants to use me for a whole week to videotape the same subject." "He sounds very manipulative," Mr. Philstein speculated. "Make sure you get paid in full for the last job before you do anything more," Mr. Philstein rightfully advised me.

When Mr. Weinberg called back the next day, I told him I would charge him a flat rate of $500 per day plus travel, report writing, and expenses. He agreed to my terms without trying to counter-offer. He said that he would Federal Express partial payment for the last job if I could begin the new job immediately. Believing him, I agreed. By the following morning, I was back in Dog Patch, ready to film Mr. Allen.

The Second Surveillance Job on Mr. Allen
Mr. Weinberg had stipulated that he wanted me to videotape the subject and/or his residence for ten seconds every hour (the same instructions he had stipulated for the first assignment). I explained to him that, under the circumstances, I did not believe it was in the best interest of his client to have me videotape so frequently because Mr. Allen would certainly become suspicious. Instead, I suggested that I spend a lot of time interacting with Mr. Allen's landlord and landlady, thereby winning their trust and confidence that I am, indeed, an investor from Barbados looking to purchase the area to build time-share units. Mr. Weinberg agreed that my strategy would be effective under the circumstances.

I arrived on Saturday morning at about 9:30 a.m. and, to my surprise, Mr. Allen was just exiting his front door and heading for his landlord's house. I quickly pulled over and videotaped Mr. Allen departing and returning. For the next two days, however, there was no sign of Mr. Allen. By Sunday evening, I felt that I should not have captured those first few moments on videotape. It gave me away, and Mr. Allen, I believed, was smarter than one would imagine.

On Monday morning, I, therefore, contacted Mr. Weinberg and suggested that I call it quits. "As long as I'm staying at his landlord's trailer, Mr. Allen is going to stay inside," I told Mr. Weinberg.

Mr. Weinberg was not happy. He screamed, yelled, told me I was calling him too early in the morning, suggested that I try to make something happen, and then slammed down the receiver, telling me I should call him back at a more decent hour.

Now, obviously, all of the various times that I called him for directives and heard his yelling, raging voice did not motivate me to do a very good job. From what Mr. Weinberg was saying, he simply wanted video footage of Mr. Allen's home, whether there was any action or not. With that kind of directive, I could simply sit in clear, plain view in front of Mr. Allen's residence and blatantly videotape, knowing full well that he would stay inside. I started to feel as if I was really working for Mr. Allen's lawyer — with Mr. Weinberg's blessings!

I returned to the scene and took my 9:30 a.m. duty shot. It was a bright, sunny day, and I noticed that there was a lot of light coming into my camera, in fact, so much light that I could barely see the subject's house. Something was wrong with my brand new camera and I couldn't determine what it was. After taking the front, back, and side shots, I stopped at the end of the dirt road to examine my camera more carefully and ascertain what the problem might be. Alas! I discovered that I had accidentally left the lens open to night vision, and, hence, the picture was over-exposed. Having just had my ass chewed out by Mr. Weinberg for the umpteenth time, I really didn't feel motivated to retake the 9:30 a.m. shots. Why should I go out of my way to retake videotape of a barren scene? I decided I would just go catch some breakfast and return in an hour, and then retake the shot. While still toying with the decision, however, I found myself rounding the bend and ready to take another boring shot of Mr. Allen's property.

Lo and behold! There was Mr. Allen right before my eyes! He was in the process of unlocking his van, walking to open his gate, bending down to pet one of his dogs! I pulled up on the dirt road parallel to his driveway and began blatantly videotaping him! I thought, "What do I have to lose?" It was the last day of the investigation, and I was convinced that he "knew" I was not really an investor from Barbados, so I might as well get what I can.

Mr. Allen quickly noticed that I was, indeed, videotaping him. He continued to unlock his gate and then enter his truck. As he stepped inside, he looked squarely at me and tossed his hands up while shrugging, as if to say, "What's up?" So I waved at him and blew him a kiss. He looked a bit taken aback by this behavior, but he decided to wave back. I waved again and, again, he returned the gesture. Suddenly, he decided to exit his truck and walk over to me. I rolled down my driver's window, and the conversation began (the camera rolling the entire time).

"What's up?"

"So, are you ready to move?"

"You really are an investor from Barbados?"

"Why, certainly."

"Then, why are you videotaping me, my property, so much?"

"I'm videotaping everyone. You just haven't noticed."

There was a beat of silence. He paced back and forth on the passenger side of my van.

"Besides, you're so cute," I said, panning him from head to toe.

He laughed, shrugged, and started walking away.

"Where're you headed?" I inquired.

"I'm going to pick up my mail."

"Great! I'll follow you!" I announced.

And away we went.

On the ride to the post office, I seriously wondered who was bluffing whom. My heart was pounding heavily, and I started to doubt if the camera had really been on "record." In fact, this startling thought alarmed me so much, that I checked the viewer while at a stop light. I sighed with relief when I saw the smiling face of Mr. Allen waving at me.

When we arrived at the post office, Mr. Allen stepped out of his truck and headed inside. The small town post office is adjacent to a convenience store, and there were several customers entering and exiting both establishments, taking notice of my blatant videotaping of Mr. Allen as he entered and exited the post office. All the while, I'm talking with him, openly "flirting" with him.

"You certainly are the cutest man in Springtown," I began. He hung his head low and laughed as he headed into the post office. "Are you married?"

"Yes."

"For how long?"

"Twelve years."

"You got the twelve year itch?"

"No. Not today." He laughed.

"How 'bout we do lunch?"

"Sorry. Not today."

During this conversation, Mr. Allen entered the post office, bent down, unlocked his mail box, retrieved his mail, stood up, used his right hand (the hand that supposedly does not work) to open a letter, and re-entered his truck.

After Mr. Allen left the scene, I was so excited, I called my husband. "Honey! I got him! I got him! I got him!" It was almost too good to be true. "Mr. Weinberg will certainly be impressed," I stated.

But the adventure had just begun.

For two days, I had basically been just schmoozing with Mr. Allen's landlord and landlady.

Roy and Annie Eastland are very obese people who live in a run down house adjacent to Mr. Allen's rental home. Roy is a big guy, about 450 pounds, with most of his teeth missing. One tooth, the bottom front, Roy tried to remove a few years back with a pair of pliers but he couldn't get the damn thing all the way out. Now, he uses his tongue all day long to play with it and wobble it from front to back. There's a tattoo on his right hand he received while in prison. "Happy go lucky," it says, and Roy loves to tell a good story. During the two days we spent together, I listened to many of his tales from the joint, and also stories about when he was young, rich, and good-looking.

"Back in my good-looking days, I used to get the best dames. One night I picked up this high class dame in my Cadillac and we drove off. I noticed she was wearing some mighty fine smelling perfume, so I sniffed the air and asked her, 'What's that smell?' She replied, 'It's *Evening in Paris,* $150 a half ounce.' A few blocks later, I realized I had to pass gas. I just couldn't hold it no more. So, I let it seep out, silent but deadly, and I sniffed the air and said, 'What's that smell? Oh, yes, it's sweet potatoes, five dollars a bushel.'"

The big man continued along in this manner, entertaining my partner and me for hours on end. The whole time, we thought we had convinced him that we truly were interested in buying his and other folks' properties. While I embroidered a bedspread, my partner, D.H., periodically got up from the table and walked over to Mr. Allen's house and took a couple of video shots. Back at the Eastland's residence, I introduced the couple to vegetarian cooking. On Saturday, I prepared vegetarian chili for the family; on Sunday, Mr. Eastland ate tofu for the first time.

"This stuff ain't too bad," he said, swallowing his first bite. "It's better than I thought it would be."

"And it's good for you," I said. "Won't cause you heartburn."

The big man was impressed. He could see that I was truly and genuinely interested in his health. I wrote down a few more recipes for his wife. We played cards, swapped stories, watched TV.

Around 4:30 p.m. on Monday, while sitting in Mr. Eastland's house just passing the time, embroidering in between getting my hourly shots of Mr. Allen's property, Roy entered his kitchen and nudged me gently.

"You'd better go get your camera right now," he said. "Your man is out there cleaning his yard."

I was dumbfounded. Should I admit that, yes, I really am a P.I.? Or should I deny? While I hesitated, Roy continued talking.

"Come on," he said, holding out his hand. "Give me $100 right now and I'll keep him out there. You can get all the video footage you want."

"I can't do that," I told him. "But I'll pay you $50 to change my oil and fix my right turn signal."

"It's a deal," he said.

I headed over to my trailer, but by the time I returned with my camera, Mr. Allen was headed off to the dump.

"Don't worry," Roy said. "He'll be back. And we'll get something even better," Roy insisted. I still wondered whose side he really was on. He ordered me to hide out in his van where I could get a clear and inconspicuous view of his tenant's yard. Within minutes, Mr. Allen was indeed back and Roy was talking with him. Soon, the two of them were cleaning Mr. Allen's yard. Things had to be moved for, you know, the "investors from Barbados." They didn't want to see any trash in anyone's yard. Ah, yes, the investors. Mr. Allen told Roy how I had been coming on to him. Roy reassured him that I had, in fact, confided that I was harboring a bit of a crush on Mr. Allen.

Roy ordered Mr. Allen to move old pieces of furniture, bedposts, a coffee table, and a bench from his yard. He'd pick up the item, walk it over to the fence, and hurl it over. I couldn't believe I was actually videotaping this scene. How could Mr. Allen not know that he was being "had" by his landlord?

Soon, it was evening. At 10:30 p.m., I took my last shot and headed back to Gainesville. All in all, I'd had a marvelous time. I'd feasted on vegetarian food, listened to many entertaining stories, went for many walks in the night air, embroidered a bedspread, got my oil changed, and, of course, videotaped Mr. Allen.

I later found out that three other P.I.s had attempted to get video footage of Mr. Allen. None had succeeded. This was truly a tricky job. If I had not befriended Mr. Allen's landlord, I certainly would not have been successful, either.

The Aftermath — Dealing With Mr. Weinberg

But the job was still not done. Back in Gainesville, I discovered that no check had arrived by Federal Express, as Mr. Weinberg had promised. Instead, Mr. Weinberg had one of his thugs call me the next morning.

"Ms. Woodhull, why didn't you call our office last night?"

It was just another "tale" from Mr. Weinberg's office.

"Sorry, bud, but the game is up," I told him.

"Ms. Woodhull. You know you are supposed to report out."

"I did. You know it. Where's my check?"

"Excuse me!?"

"You heard me. No check. No videotape. It's as simple as that."

Mr. Weinberg and his thug then spent the next three days trying to obtain the videotape without paying me. They threatened to sue me, call the state of Florida, have my license revoked, drive up to Gainesville to obtain it, etc. Finally, my attorney friend spoke with Mr. Weinberg and the next day, a check for the full amount arrived by Federal Express. I had learned a lot on this job. Not only did I videotape a difficult subject, but I also learned how to handle a difficult big time player and win. Now, it was time to market to the insurance companies myself.

Points to remember: What made this investigation a success?

1. **Remember: Even folks in backwoods can spot a P.I.** Don't go onto the scene in a dark tinted van with binoculars and a camcorder and expect no one to notice you. Instead, come up with a pretext. In this case, we used three pretexts: (1) Visiting with the Lowmans; (2) Investors from Barbados; (3) Investigating the drug dealers (the pretext we used on the Lowmans).

2. **Interact with people in the neighborhood.** Get them to know you and to trust you. Even if they suspect you're undercover, they'll help you, if they like you enough.

3. **Always listen to their stories.** Listening is one of the best P.I. tools. During the 1930s, Dale Carnegie, author of *How to Win Friends and Influence People,* recommended lis-

tening as one of the best tools for getting people to like you.

4. **Interact with as many people as possible in the neighborhood.** As the word spreads, the subject will be more inclined to exit his house and engage in self-incriminating outdoor activities.

Points to Remember: Working for the Big Guys

1. **Don't let them intimidate you.** Many large firms use intimidation tactics to try to bargain down the price or not pay at all. Let them scream, rage, and threaten to have your license revoked. If you do a good job, you'll get your money in the end.

2. **Even better yet, get your money up front (at least one third).**

3. **It is illegal to try to get out of a bill by using threats and intimidation.** The big guys know this, but a gentle reminder cannot hurt.

Here Comes the Bride

A plastic surgeon was about to be sued by a former patient who claimed that he had maimed her and destroyed all of her joy in life when he disfigured her face. At 16, she had been in a major car wreck which had misaligned her jaw. The surgeon had reconstructed her jaw line, but she was claiming that he did a terrible job. Her life ruined, she was seeking a million dollars.

It just so happened that a nurse who works for the plastic surgeon discovered that the 19-year-old was about to get married on Saturday. The plastic surgeon wanted to know if I'd be willing to attend the reception and get good video footage close-ups of her allegedly maimed jaw line.

For this job, I took along my husband, and my partner, D.H. We dressed in wedding guest attire and we took along two video cameras and a still camera.

The wedding was quite upscale and when we arrived, we headed straight for the food and beverage area. The plastic surgeon's wife had also wrapped up a very special gift for us to present to the bride — a somewhat symbolic gesture, indeed: a toaster.

While the bride danced her first dance with her father, we oohed and aahed over her gown, her gloves, her bridal headpiece, while we videotaped her. We talked with the guests, drank champagne, danced the Macarena.

While D.H. videotaped the bride with "no joy in her life" dancing the Electric Slide, I.J. and I walked around the premises taking still photos. When the bride and groom cut the cake, we were there to zoom in with our cameras and witness her "joyless face."

Turns out this was one of the prettiest, happiest brides one would ever want to see. We even interviewed her twin sister at one point who declared on videotape, "My sister is, indeed, the prettiest bride in the whole world. She's beautiful because she looks just like me."

Indeed, the two young women were model-quality knockouts.

As the wedding reception progressed, we did notice that the bride started smiling differently. At first, her beaming smile was straight, but a few hours later, when she noticed her unrecognized guests were constantly videotaping her, she would droop the one corner of her mouth and bite her teeth together.

After about three hours, the bride's father approached D.H. and wanted to know who the hell we were. D.H. directed the man to me. I said we were surprise musicians and when would we be able to perform? We walked to our van to get our musical instruments and never returned.

Oh, my. The bride was busted — right on her wedding day.

Points to Remember: What made this assignment a success?

1. **We appeared to be having a good time.** Turns out everyone knew one another at this wedding reception. There were no distant, out of town guests. But, by playing the role of happy guests and bringing a present, we fit right in — for a while.

2. **We weren't afraid to videotape.** Even if we had been invited to leave sooner, we felt certain that we had already obtained enough footage to bust the bride. Not even a scar was visible on her left jaw line, where the surgery had been performed.

3. **We are, in fact, musicians.** We did, in fact, bring musical instruments and we were ready to perform if we had been questioned upon our arrival. We were prepared to say that one of the guests had hired us to play a few tunes but that person wished to remain anonymous until after the wedding reception. We were going to say that when the gift we brought was opened, it would be clear who hired us to perform as musicians.

Although we did not have to use this pretext, we were ready and willing to play a few tunes. If we had started off in this manner, we naturally would have been invited to stay and enjoy ourselves. During this time period, we would have videotaped and snapped pictures for "the secret guest who hired us."

Watermelon Man

When Charlie Bower, the "watermelon farmer," accused J.P. Crakes, the "logger man," of giving him "whiplash," no one was surprised. These two good ol' boys had been battling each other for more than 30 years. J.P.'s been raging mad for decades — ever since Charlie had an affair with his wife. Several years ago, Charlie claimed that J.P.'s logger boys stole a truck of his watermelons. Then Charlie claimed that J.P. poured a bucket of chartreuse paint on Charlie's brand new pickup truck.

Now, it was time for Charlie to finally settle the score. It was a quiet Sunday morning when Charlie stopped dead smack in the middle of a lonely, country road while J.P. was driving behind him.

No witnesses.

Whiplash.

Ha! Charlie chuckled to himself. He believed he had a foolproof plan. No private investigator would catch Charlie this season working out in the watermelon fields. No. He'd let his boys do all the hard labor. In Charlie's mind, it was a foolproof plan. He'd have the logger boy "over a barrel." (No pun intended, ahem!)

Enter YOURS TRULY, a.k.a. World's Greatest P.I., collector of Weird Ass Stories about Weird Ass People. Certainly I could pretext that I am a freelance writer in search of a good story for watermelon season. Wait a second! I really **am** a freelance writer some of the time! Well! This should be an easy assignment!

My first stop was at the local feed store.

"Hi!" I said. I was wearing a black and white polka-dotted tight mini dress with a black baseball cap, my pony tail pulled through the back of the cap.

"Do you guys know any watermelon farmers around here? I'm looking to freelance a story."

Three names and addresses later, I was on my way to Charlie's farm.

Charlie was out running errands, his helpers informed me. He had to go to the post office and the bank, but he'd be back shortly. His employees gave me plenty of good watermelon stories to help pass the time. I took a lot of notes, like a good freelance writer would do.

Enter Charlie. Sweaty, short. Balding. But definitely **not** suffering from whiplash.

His first question: "Where'd you get **my** name and number?"

Well, I already had **that** question covered, now didn't I?

"From the feed store," I replied. Charlie looked instantly more trusting.

I interviewed Charlie for about an hour. Now it was time for the big test.

"Charlie," I said. "Let's you and me go out to the watermelon patches and take some pictures of you with your prize-winning, big watermelons."

"It sounds like fun," Charlie replied.

And so we entered his pickup truck. His eight-year-old son rode in the back.

The pictures I snapped were beautiful, scenic. The kind of photos I **really** could have sold to a trade magazine.

"Now, let's get a little more artistic, Charlie," I told my new watermelon pal. Charlie was jovial. (I really kinda **liked** this guy.)

"Okay. Let's put your son up on your shoulders. Now turn your body so that your back is facing me, and look over your right shoulder."

"Smile, Charlie, smile."

Then there was **the** best photo — Charlie holding his prize 57 pound watermelon high over his head, his neck turned 180 degrees as he smiled for the camera.

"Say 'cheese,' Charlie."

"Cheese."

Employee From Hell

Ms. Latosha Henderson came to work with her arm in a sling. She handed the human resources director a note from her doctor indicating that she would not be able to work for the next six months — at the very least.

Once again, Ms. Henderson had been declared "disabled." It was not the first time she had been excused from work for a medical-related disability. In fact, it was the **13th** time in thirteen years that Ms. Henderson had managed to find a way to take advantage of the company's 100 percent disability insurance coverage policy. There had been alleged broken bones, sprained ankles, neck and back injuries, and a variety of other ailments over the years that kept. Latosha from coming to work. On average, she had worked one-third of every year and taken off for medical-related reasons nine months of every year.

Five years ago, the company had attempted to fire her. But Latosha sued the company for gender and racial discrimination. Part of the out-of-court settlement included reinstating Latosha and giving her $30,000. Since that time, it appeared that she had "upped the ante." Her latest disability claim had been signed by a plastic surgeon — a hand specialist, although no surgery had been ordered. This seemed curious in itself. But when the company discovered that Latosha had also been receiving full medical disability benefits from the U.S. Army Reserves, they decided to investigate the "double-dipping." That's when Snow Chemical Company contacted Yours Truly — The World's Greatest P.I. The new human resources manager, Mr. Guy Quinn, hired me to observe Ms. Henderson for a period of one week to determine if her arm was, indeed, temporarily paralyzed, as Ms. Henderson and her plastic surgeon doctor had been claiming.

Day One
The first day of an investigation is always the most difficult. I call this the "foundation day." First, I check out the situation. This job was going to require many long hours of surveillance, so I naturally wanted to see where I could find a good place to hide out and watch the woman with the allegedly paralyzed arm. The scene I discovered was rather dismal. She resided in a large, beautiful home set back off of a highway. Across the street from her residence was an open field. Next door to her on one side was forest with no clear view of her home. On the other side was a row of trees parallel to a driveway, which led to her neighbor's wooden, dilapidated home. While Ms. Henderson lived in luxury, her neighbor lived in a cottage-type shack with two dogs tied up in the yard. For the next two days, I drove up and down the highway spot-checking to see when the neighbor would be at home. My only hope was that I could befriend the neighbor, perhaps rent a room from him or rent the acre of property in front of his house and put a camper on that piece of land from which I could then conduct surveillance. For three days, however, there was no sign of the neighbor. Finally, I checked my computer records and discovered that the neighbor was a clergyman and that the neighborhood is all black. This made it doubly difficult to get anything accomplished, since it would look very suspicious for a white woman to be hanging out in the neighborhood in a van for

long periods of time. But as I thought and thought about the situation, I finally came up with a plan.

Day Two

On the second day of the investigation, I hired one of my private investigator interns to drive by the scene with me. Lo and behold, as we drove down the highway at nearly sunset, there was Latosha out in her yard with her boyfriend and son (I had already checked out the dwelling via computer) watering the lawn, picking up debris and branches, etc. We parked in the Reverend's driveway, and while I videotaped from inside the tinted van, my intern exited the van and pretended to be feeding the dogs (he did give them water). I managed to get about 20 minutes of "Latosha Does The Yard" on film. The following morning, I called the company and was elated to tell them that I had already nailed their subject. I drove to the company and we watched the world premiere of my film.

Day Three

But the manager was disappointed. In the film, he noted, Latosha was only using her right arm. "It is her **left** arm that is allegedly paralyzed," he informed me.

I felt disheartened. First of all, I wished he had told me this information up front. Second, it now appeared that Latosha is very slick. She obviously has had experience dealing with private investigators and their antics in the past. **Or** her left arm truly was paralyzed. With five days to go, I had to come up with a new strategy and I wasn't quite sure what it would be.

Day Four

"Good morning," the caller said. "I am an information specialist for the RJW corporation.

"May I please speak to the lady of the house?"

"This is the lady of the house."

"Ma'am, we are assessing the number of Afro-American residents who are registered to vote in the upcoming primary elections to determine how we can obtain a greater voter turnout. For participating in this phone interview, we are offering a free 20-pound turkey from your local Big Ben supermarket. Would you mind taking a brief minute to answer a few questions?"

"Not at all," Ms. Henderson replied.

The Strategy

Here's what I had done. (1) I called an Afro-American girlfriend of mine who works for the insurance industry. She was willing to lend a helping hand by posing as a telephone surveyor. (2) I also contacted a friend of mine who is the manager of a Big Ben supermarket. He was willing to hand Ms. Henderson the coupon I would generate for her free turkey. He would then call me upon her arrival at the grocery store so I could videotape her loading up the buggy with her free turkey. As a bonus for her participation in the survey, we were also going to offer her a free $50 gift certificate — if she would use it immediately. That way, we could possibly videotape her placing several items in her shopping cart with her "non-functioning" arm.

During the phone interview, we learned: (1) Where she attends church, (2) That she was not interested in receiving the free turkey, but (3) Not only was she registered to vote on Tuesday, she was going to be **working** at the polls.

It Was a Long Weekend

It was a long holiday weekend prior to Tuesday, the day of the primaries. On Friday evening, I was with I.J., parked in the Reverend's driveway waiting for Latosha to come outside to do yardwork. We sat there for two and a half hours with no sign of activity... that is until the Reverend and his wife pulled into their driveway. Concerned about their un-known visitors, the Reverend, et. al., pulled up and I hung my head out of the window.

"Hi! Are you Reverend Jones?"

"Yes," replied the baffled owner.

I launched into one of my alibis, "We're new to the area and are waiting for our government housing check to come through on Tuesday, so we've been living out of our van and we were looking for a place to camp for a few days. One of your neighbors down the road said you might be able to help us... she's a friend of a friend and we've been staying in her yard, but the street light is bothering us while we sleep and we were wondering if you might be willing to rent some of your property by the road?"

"Who sent you down here?" inquired Mrs. Jones, sus-picious of these two "homeless" white people in her yard.

"Vicky, three houses down."

"We don't have anything for rent," assured the Reverend.

On to the backup alibi: "We were also wondering if we might be able to set up a boiled peanut stand on the side of the road in front of your property?"

"Why don't you do that in front of Vicky's house?" the Reverend wondered.

"They have a fence and there's not enough room," I pleaded to the uncooperative couple. I then dropped the name of another black preacher in a nearby town and asked if Reverend Jones knew her. The Reverend indicated so and seemed a little less worried. He then told me that he pastors at a church about 50 miles away, which explained his con-tinuous absence from his property over the past several days.

The couple said that they had to go to dinner and I told Reverend Jones I would stop by his house the next day to see if we could arrange a temporary living agreement on his property, though it looked bleak. We left immediately to have certified paperwork drawn up proving that we were "homeless" and had no outstanding warrants by the sheriff's department.

On Saturday morning, I went to see Reverend Jones, with my paperwork verifying that I was "homeless and harmless," only to find him running late on his way to a funeral and still not interested in offering any help to a "homeless" family living in their van. I then drove back to Vicky's yard — a timely decision, because the Reverend decided to drive intentionally in the direction of her house, do a U-turn, and drive back by, thus verifying that my story was legit.

Over the next two days, three of us drove up and down the highway spot-checking Ms. Henderson's house to see if she was going to come out and engage in yard work or any other outdoor activities. On Saturday and Sunday, she entertained relatives in her double car garage, as it was either too hot or raining outside. We went to her church on Sunday, but Ms. Henderson did not attend the services. We had just about given up hope that we would ever spot her driving a car with her "non-working" arm until Sunday afternoon.

At that time, investigator D.H. just happened to be driving down the highway when he spotted Ms. Henderson returning in her Honda Civic. He videotaped the vehicle for one second as it was turning back into the driveway, but he was not able to I.D. Ms. Henderson (although she was, indeed, the driver). Now, at least we had hope. We knew for sure that she was using her "non-working" arm.

The Heat is On

We continued driving our routes along the highway in front of the house and stopping at our designated turn-around points — Vicky's yard and an open field next to a green house. On Monday morning, as I.J. was parked in front of the green house, the owner, a stout black lady, drove up and asked him if there was some reason why he had been parking there over the past couple of days. He said he was waiting for some friends to arrive from out of town and that he was afraid they wouldn't be able to find the friend's (Vicky's) house, so he was parked out in the open so they could see him. Unconvinced, the lady asked him to not park in front of her yard and followed him back to Vicky's house. A half hour later, a deputy sheriff pulled up behind I.J. and he told the same story while a license check was performed and he was told that the lady in the green house was concerned and had made the call.

Feeling our welcome being worn out and having sat endless hours over the weekend with no success, I decided it was time to make one last risky attempt to catch Ms. Henderson on tape. As the sun began to set we would drop off D.H. along the row of trees separating Latosha's house from Reverend Jones' driveway, have him sneak into the woods and sit like a sniper with the video camera. The only problem was D.H.'s lack of camouflage attire. The only clothing we had that would help to blend his bare legs in with the trees was a dark-colored wrap-around skirt.

D.H. drew up the tight-fitting skirt around his waist and hopped out of the van with camera in hand. As he slowly entered the woods, we exited Reverend Jones' driveway only to discover that the Reverend was just a few hundred yards away from turning in! I.J. immediately sped off in the opposite direction and we watched in the rearview mirrors to see what would happen.

The Reverend's car came to a stop at about the same spot where D.H. had entered the tree line, sat for a few minutes, and then began to turn around. I told I.J. to pull into a neighbor's gated driveway and I jumped out and opened the gate, while I.J. pulled up and closed the gate behind. We pulled up near the house and sat motionless in the van, watching Reverend Jones' car coming down the highway in our direction.

The Reverend drove past the driveway we had entered and returned in the opposite direction in a minute, pulling up alongside the neighbor's yard on the opposite side of the highway. He then got out of his vehicle and walked around to stand by the passenger side, and alternated peering at our van and at the house in the yard next to him. What was going on? Had he caught D.H. on his property and was now trying to bring him back to us? We stayed still and then began to chuckle at the entire situation: Here was this ragged band of white "homeless" people terrorizing a minister in an all-black neighborhood and then he discovers a man in a skirt in the woods on his property with a video camera! What must the Reverend be thinking? What must D.H. be thinking?

After about 10 minutes, the Reverend drove off down the road and pulled into the driveway of the green house. We figured it was time to pay the piper and go rescue D.H. from the Reverend, so we headed back down the highway towards the green house, and made a quick stop by the Reverend's driveway, honking the horn, in hopes that D.H. was still there. I.J. honked while I yelled for D.H., but we saw no movement. I.J. honked the horn one final time and then D.H. appeared out of the rough. I screamed for him to hurry up as he ran as fast as he could, considering he was wearing a full-length skirt.

D.H. reached the van and I.J. floored the accelerator, pinning D.H. in the back of his seat as he was trying to close the door. He was clueless as to what the matter was, but frantic at the same time. We barreled down the highway, deciding to make our last effort the next day, when Ms. Henderson would be away from her house.

Tuesday — The Day of the Primaries

Ms. Henderson told her boss at Snow Chemical that she had an appointment with her doctor, the plastic surgeon, early on Tuesday morning. The three of us went to the medical office complex to see if we could videotape her entering or exiting the premises with her Honda Civic. There were three driveways leading into the parking lot. Each one of us staked out an entrance and then videotaped each and every car that entered and exited the premises. By 10:30 a.m., we were certain that Ms. Henderson had not shown up for her appointment.

Next, we began driving to all of the voting precincts. We got very lucky. At the second voting precinct, we spotted Ms. Henderson's Honda Civic, which indicated that she was inside the voting precinct working as a helper on voting day — just as she had indicated to the "telephone surveyor."

My heart was pounding hard. What should we do next? I called the company and the human resource director suggested that I enter the poll and see if I could volunteer for the day. I knew I would have to be a resident of the area in order to accomplish this feat. I quickly scoped out the neighborhood and noticed there was a brand new double-wide mobile home being erected across from the polling booth.

Now I Suddenly had a new Address

I knocked on the door of the mobile home. A young man, about early thirties, came to the door. I introduced myself with a big smile.

"Hi," I said. "May I come in for a minute?"

"Sure," he replied. "Anyone as attractive as you can enter my new residence. What is this all about?"

I felt I could trust the young man. I showed my badge and I.D. "Listen, I'm on a case right now. I need to pretend that

I'm living here. Can I pay you $50 to rent me a room for the day and pose as my brother-in-law?"

Lucky for me, the man agreed. I gave him a few more details to ease his mind, but not enough to tell him anything that could jeopardize the confidentiality of the case. It turns out the young man is a local disc jockey. He had just moved to the area and was interested in registering to vote. So the two of us walked over to the voting precinct (which was held in a small, Baptist church) and said we were there to register and then cast our ballots.

There were three middle-aged women sitting at a long table waiting to assist them. One of them was Ms. Henderson. My new "brother-in-law" went over to her and heartily shook her "non-working" hand with gusto. While he cast his votes, I explained that I had left eggs boiling on the stove back at the house and would come back a little later. Of course, I did not return.

It was a Long Day

For the rest of the day, I sat in my van waiting for Ms. Henderson to come out and drive away in her five-speed stick shift car. This is where job dedication really comes into play. During the long day, I was forced to use an empty Slurpy cup for liquid body waste elimination and then periodically dump the cup out the window. A couple of people saw me waiting in my van and stopped to ask me what was up. I said I was working for a surveying company that was counting the number of people who came to vote for the day — how many men, women, black, white. I even kept count just to show the curious stoppers.

Around 6 p.m., I.J. came and joined me on the scene in another vehicle. Now, there were two of us ready to capture Ms. Henderson as she exited the precinct at the end of the day. We videotaped everyone who entered and exited the premises, since we had no idea when Ms. Henderson was going to leave. Lucky for us, the very last person to come in and vote for the evening before the polls closed was the disc jockey's wife. He had already informed his wife as to what was going on. While inside the polling center, she observed Ms. Henderson folding up the voting booths with her "nonworking" arm. Now, we had a witness, at the very least.

Around 7:30 p.m., Ms. Henderson did exit the voting precinct and unlocked her vehicle with her "non-functioning" arm. She then tugged at the seat belt with this same arm and drove off. We videotaped the entire scene from two angles.

Prior to driving home, Ms. Henderson stopped at a convenience store where she exited her vehicle twice and entered the store twice, buying lottery tickets on both occasions. The entire transaction was videotaped. Three times in all, we observed her tugging on her seat belt, locking it in place, unlocking her vehicle, putting the stick shift in reverse, forward, and then pulling away. Each time she exited the convenience store, she was clearly I.D.ed. I knew at this point that she clearly had been making fraudulent claims regarding her arm. The videotapes we had were enough to get her into big time trouble.

Back at Snow Chemical the Following Morning

The following morning, I drove to Snow Chemical and three of us viewed the tapes. The human resource director and manager were extremely pleased.

A few days later, I called to get the rest of the story.

First, Ms. Henderson was contacted by phone to see how she was doing. She indicated that she had been too sick to keep her doctor's appointment but that she was scheduled to see him the very next day and would report back to the human resource director at Snow Chemical just as soon as her doctor met with her the following day.

The following afternoon, Ms. Henderson called Snow Chemical's human resource director and told him that her doctor said she was so sick that she could not even bathe herself. She could not even pick up a hair brush to brush her own hair. The doctor suggested that she hire someone to come in and bathe her and brush her hair for her. At that point, the human resource director asked her to come in for a brief interview.

At the interview, the human resource director questioned Ms. Henderson as to her whereabouts on primary day. During the questioning, Ms. Henderson caught on that "something was up." At one point during the interview, she stood up and announced that she was sick of working for Snow Chemical and that she would like to resign. Her resignation was immediately accepted — with glee!

The company saved at least a quarter of a million dollars in benefits that they were going to have to pay her. Ms. Henderson actually got off very lightly. She could have been prosecuted for fraud and "double-dipping." However, the company was simply relieved that they would be rid of this "employee from hell."

Once again, I am compelled to tell those of you who are in charge of hiring others that it is much easier and cheaper to investigate a potential employee up front than to hire someone and then be sued and harassed for 13 years. It had been a long nightmare, but this employee from hell was finally gone.

Chapter Six
You're Served

Serving court papers or subpoenas is ideal work for P.I.s. In Gainesville, court documents are delivered by deputy sheriffs in uniform, which may forewarn the recipient who might want to avoid being served.

How's This Color?

A man was attempting to sue a painter for not completing a job, which he had paid for in-full up-front. Besides, the painting the man had done was not acceptable. Every time the sheriff attempted to serve the painter, he did not open his door. The painter's unhappy customer, with the aid of his attorney, contacted me to serve the painter.

It turns out the painter lived two blocks from my own home, so it was easy for me to check periodically throughout the day and see when the man's white van was in his driveway. Finally, on the fourth day of checking, I spotted his van.

I called the painter by phone and told him I had just purchased the duplex down the block and across the street from him. How soon would he be able to meet me there and give me an estimate for a paint job? He said he would meet me there immediately.

I drove to Home Depot and picked up some paint color tab samples. Then, when I met the painter, I first pulled the sample tabs out of my pocket and asked him which color he thought would hold up the best, since this was going to be a rental property. As he examined the colors, clipboard in hand, I pulled the hidden papers out of my large coat pocket.

"And what do you think of this?" I inquired. As I placed the papers on top of his clipboard, I began walking away. "You are hereby served. You are to appear in court on January 3 at 10 a.m." The man stood there for a moment staring at me, staring at the paint tabs, then glancing back down at the papers. Yes, indeed, he had been served.

Will the Real Dave Sheraton Please Stand up?

An attorney contacted me and wanted me to serve a subpoena to a Mr. Dave Sheraton. Checking the local phone book, he had obtained what he thought was the man's address. I went to that address and discovered it was a generic address for about 200 trailers in a large trailer park. Lucky for me, I knew someone who used to reside in that trailer park, so I went to the park office to begin my investigation.

"Hey! How ya doin'?"

"Pretty good! How 'bout yourself?"

"You remember me?"

"You look kinda familiar."

"I used to live here with Eddie Greer. You remember him, don't you?"

"Oh, yeah! How's he doin' these days?"

"Real good! He recently got remarried."

"He did!?"

"Real nice girl. Eddie got really lucky."

"Sounds like it."

"And what about my old friend, Dave Sheraton? Which number trailer does he stay in? I forget. And I have some money here that I've owed him for a long time. He'll be happy to see me."

"You just missed him. He moved out just about one week ago."

"No foolin'! Where'd he go?"

"I don't know. Even if I did know, I wouldn't be at liberty to tell you."

"Well, that's too bad. If you hear from him, tell him I finally got his money for him."

"And what's your name?"

"Just tell him, his old friend, 'The Brunette.' He'll know who you're talking about."

"Sure thing."

Now, there were two strategies I could have taken at this point. (1) I wasn't expecting that Dave Sheraton would have moved. I thought the generic address to the trailer park simply meant I had to be clever enough to discover which trailer was his. If he had, in fact, still lived there, and the office had refused to give me the specific number, I simply would have knocked on every door asking for him until I found him. I also could have asked his old neighbors where he might have moved to. (2) A second strategy, and one that was quicker and easier, was to go back to my office and contact the utilities company. Perhaps they had a new address in his name. I decided to try the latter approach first, and then go back to the trailer park, if it became necessary.

Back at my office, I contacted the electric company and was immediately given his new apartment number and also the fact that he works at Wal-Mart. So I called the attorney and said, "If he's at work right now, do you want me to serve him right at Wal-Mart?" The attorney said that would be fine.

There are two Wal-Marts in Gainesville. I called the first one and asked my usual "assumption question."

"Can you connect me with Dave Sheraton?"

"One moment, please."

While waiting on hold, I wondered what I might say to him if and when he should pick up the phone. Again, I did not assume he was really there. I had to hear his actual voice to verify that he really works at that location.

I stayed on hold long enough that I decided to call the other Wal-Mart on the other line.

Again, I asked, "Can you connect me with Dave Sheraton?"

This time I was connected immediately, without any delay. A male voice said, "Produce."

I was a little startled, but I knew I had to think fast. "Is this produce?"

"Yes."

"Is Dave Sheraton there?"

"This is Dave Sheraton."

"Oh. Are the raspberries still on sale?"

"Raspberries? We don't carry raspberries."

"Well, I don't know what you call them. Those little red things."

"I don't know what you're talking about, ma'am."

"Well, how late are you going to be there?"

"I'll be here until 4 p.m."

"Okay. I'll just come down in person."

I checked my watch. It was now 3:30 p.m. I knew I would not be able to make it across town by 4 p.m. So, I decided to go directly to his new apartment and just sit on his front porch until he came home. I acted on the hunch that he would want to come home — even if just briefly — after getting off from a hard day's work. Then, I would simply touch the papers to his chest and announce, "You're served," after verifying that it was him.

It turned out that he lived in an upstairs apartment, so I used the wait time to walk up and down the stairs repeatedly, thereby getting a bit of exercise for the day. Sure enough, by 4:30 p.m., a tall man with a dark mustache was walking up the stairs, carrying mail in his left hand and a bag of groceries in the right.

"Dave Sheraton?" I inquired, as he ascended the stairs.

"Yes."

"You are hereby served." And I handed him the papers.

I continued down the steps and whispered "sorry" under my breath.

"Wait a second! Wait a second!" he protested. "Yes, I am Dave Sheraton, but I'm not the right Dave Sheraton that you are looking for!"

I made an about-face from the bottom of the stairs and gave him a smirky look.

"Ah, come on."

"No! I'm serious! I can prove it!" he said. "There's another Dave Sheraton who works at the **other** Wal-Mart! **That's** the guy you're looking for!"

"How do I know you're telling me the truth? I'm looking for a Dave Sheraton who used to work at K-Mart."

"Yeah. I know. That's **him!** He used to work at K-Mart and now he works for Wal-Mart. I'll even take you there and introduce you to him!"

The man sounded sincere. I called my attorney client from Dave Sheraton's upstairs apartment.

"Do you think he's telling you the truth?" the attorney inquired.

"Could be."

Right then, Dave Sheraton exited his bedroom with award plaques he had received over the years for his good service at Wal-Mart.

He explained, "One cannot work simultaneously for Wal-Mart and K-Mart. I would have been fired."

Next thing I know, I was in Dave Sheraton's car on my way to the other Wal-Mart in search of an Afro-American named Dave Sheraton.

As we drove to Wal-Mart, Dave Sheraton explained to me that he had just been through a divorce after 11 years of marriage. His wife had left him for another man. They had been to court many times. He assumed when I was attempting to serve him that it was more court battles with his ex-wife.

We walked into Wal-Mart and the search for the real Dave Sheraton began. We cruised the aisles and finally Dave Sheraton said to me in whispered tones, "That's him, right over there, stocking the candy shelves."

"Are you sure?"

"Yes! I'm positive!"

I approached the man, "Dave Sheraton?"

"Yes?"

"You are hereby served." And I placed the papers on his chest.

He glanced at them as I was walking away and said, "Wait a second! This ain't me! It's **him**!" And he pointed to the first Dave Sheraton.

"No, it's not!"

"Well, it ain't me, either. That ain't my name." And the second Dave Sheraton took a state of Florida I.D. out of his pocket (not a driver's license) and showed me that his name was Calvin Brown.

"He must have changed his name!" Dave Sheraton protested.

By now, the store undercover shopper was curious to know what was up. He came over and flashed his badge, "May I help you?"

"Listen. I'm an undercover investigator, too. I'm just trying to get a guy served. Which one of these guys is Dave Sheraton?"

He pointed at my first guy.

"But it ain't me! I swear!"

We left the store. Now, Mr. Sheraton had another idea. As we drove back to his apartment, he remembered that there was a guy who has a Little Debbie vendor route who used to know and work with Dave Sheraton back when he was a Little Debbie vendor also. We re-entered Dave Sheraton's apartment and he called the man's answering machine. "Listen, Fred, when you get in, could you give me a call? I'm trying to get a hold of Dave Sheraton."

My buddy Dave Sheraton now claimed that he had to go pick up his kids for visiting privileges. "I gotta go," he stated, but when he calls me, I'll be sure to call you with the info."

Dave Sheraton never called back, but I did manage to obtain the number for Fred, the Little Debbie driver. Fred claimed that he hadn't seen Dave Sheraton in years and that the guy had been fired for stealing Little Debbie products.

I called back my attorney client and he spoke directly with Fred. Calling me back, he said, "Call off the investigation. If Dave Sheraton is that dishonest, I don't want him for a witness."

In the end, I wondered, "Who was the real Dave Sheraton?"

I suspect it was the first guy.

Have a Nice Flight!

A woman wanted me to serve her ex-boyfriend with court papers. Attempts by the Sheriff's department were unsuccessful. The man had been ducking out, knowing that in a short while, he would be leaving for South America.

I called the airlines and posed as him, using his name, saying that I had lost my airline ticket and needed to reconfirm the time and date of my flight. Sure enough, the information was given to me.

Hence, it was just a matter of showing up at the airport the time and date of his departing flight. There he was, with his parents, just happy as a lark that he was heading off to South America for three months of fun in the sun. Lucky for me, his flight was delayed. It took me a while to pick him out from the crowd, but after about half an hour of observation, I spotted what appeared to be the man, based upon the photos his ex-girlfriend sent me.

I approached him in a very friendly matter.

"Taylor Black?"

"Yep. That's me!" he announced proudly.

"You are hereby served." And I placed the papers on his chest.

"Drop them!" his father yelled. But it was too late, and they knew it. As I walked away, I saw them picking up and reading the papers.

The woman went to court, got her money in full, plus court costs. Justice was rendered because this subject was successfully served.

When Computers Fail...

An attorney contacted me because his attempts at locating a witness to be subpoenaed led to dead ends. The subject had quit her job, moved with no forwarding address, and had no utilities in her name. I simply went to her neighbor's house and said that I was there to drop off the cosmetics she had ordered, but that she had moved. I asked if the neighbor could help me as I flaunted my cosmetics bag and attempted to solicit the neighbor by displaying a catalog for them to order from. I gave the neighbor a free perfume sample and she gave me the new address and new place of employment.

Chapter Seven
Pre-Litigation

Conducting groundwork investigations can help clients determine if their cause is worth taking to court. Additionally, P.I.s can find out things, which may discredit witnesses, thereby providing information in criminal defense cases.

I Want a Face Lift

A plastic surgeon was curious to know what his competition was saying about him. It was rumored that one doctor was telling clients horrible things about the good surgeon. The surgeon hired me to see what his competitor might say about him if I posed as a potential patient. The report appears below.

TO: Dr. and Mrs. Franklin
FROM: Dr. Angela V. Woodhull, Private Investigator

Well! I wasn't quite sure if I would be successful pulling this one off! But, alas, I have done a better job than one would even imagine.

This report contains enough information that if you desire to file a lawsuit against Dr. Durrel for defamation of character, you certainly would be able to do so. Also, it works to your advantage that Dr. Durrel is fully aware that I am a licensed private investigator. There were no pretexts involved in my consultation discussion with him on this date.

Some background, before I cover the content of today's consultation meeting. During the past five years, I have consulted with several plastic surgeons. However, when it comes to actually going under the knife, I have been extremely reluctant. However, when I met Mrs. Franklin during the Eighth Judicial annual conference, I felt confident that I would eventually use the services of Dr. Franklin. After winning the $100 facial, I decided to save that special gift for my birthday and then discuss eyelid surgery and bartering at that time. Since I knew this was my plan, I did decide to consult with a few other plastic surgeons between the time I won the facial and the time of my birthday. On August 18, I paid for a $35 consultation with Dr. Durrel. I was not impressed with the man at that time, but I did hand him one of my P.I. business cards at that time, and so he knew that I was a P.I. In this report, I will describe both of my visits to his office. It really was beneficial that I saw him previously. Having already established "rapport" during our first consultation, Dr. Durrel was more than willing to be straightforward in his opinions of his competitors during this second consultation.

Since he knows I am a P.I., his attorney can never claim that he was "tricked" into speaking to me under the false premise that I was "just a potential client." He was made fully aware on August 18, 1999 that I am a licensed P.I. Therefore, anything to which I testify in a court of law is completely legitimate.

My first contact with Dr. Durrel's office was on the phone with his "pricing consultant," a woman named Julie. Julie is in her early fifties. She is heavyset, but she is quite personable and tells potential clients that she has had many procedures performed on herself and that she has worked for Dr. Durrel for 14 years, and that he has the best reputation in town. She told me that it is highly unusual for a plastic surgeon to keep his staff for as long as his staff has been with him, and the long-term employment is further testimony to Dr. Durrel's fine reputation. Julie, herself, has had liposuction, which brought her down from a size 18 to a size 14 jean. She has also had a facelift and eyelid surgery. She is not healthy looking, and when you meet her in person, she appears to be about a size 22. So, by phone her sales pitch is much more effective. By phone, she also took a lot of time to tell me about her mother's quadruple bypass heart surgery, which saved her mother's life. This also established rapport because my own mother was about to have that same procedure performed upon her.

FIRST VISIT. The wait in the waiting room was not long. There were about three other people present. The inside rooms are rather drab, with dark chocolate brown carpet on the floors and drab beige walls with pictures on them. Dr. Durrel appears to be prematurely gray. We talked about every procedure possible and, in the end, he recommended eyelid surgery and having my lips enlarged. Next, I met Julie in person. After handing me a price sheet (attached), she did confide in me that Dr. Franklin is not to be trusted. She said that a woman died because of a liposuction procedure he performed on her.

I did not schedule any procedure, and chalked up the $35 to a learning experience. I left one of my P.I. business cards with the front desk receptionist.

SECOND VISIT. I called Dr. Durrel's office at approximately 10 a.m. and asked to speak directly with Julie. I asked if she remembered me and she said that she did. I said that I had seen a few other plastic surgeons in town and that I was still confused, but I thought I might have Dr. Durrel perform the eyelid procedures. She said I would be charged an additional $35 for a second consultation and that I could come in that very same day at 1:45 p.m. Checking her calendar again, she said I could come immediately. I said I would be there in about half an hour. Prior to going to Dr. Durrel's office, I stopped at the Lane Health Center and obtained one of Dr. Mack's business cards, since I also had a consultation with him regarding eyelid surgery back in 1997.

I arrived at Dr. Durrel's waiting room at approximately 10:30 a.m., as scheduled. I waited for about 20 minutes. During this time, I overheard a conversation from the receptionist saying that a patient that was currently in their waiting room, a Mr. James Kenwood, was being sent immediately over to a Dr. Robert's office for some kind of immediate treatment. After Mr. Kenwood left with another man, the waiting room was completely empty. There appeared to be no one else inside except for the front desk receptionist, Julie, and a woman named Pamela, and, of course, Dr. Durrel.

Pamela ushered me back to the same room where I had been seen by Dr. Durrel on October 28. She took my chart and put it inside the slot on the hall wall and closed the door behind her. When no one was looking, I opened the door and quickly read my chart, which indicated that I have an aging, drooping face and am in need of eyelid surgery and enlargement of my lips. While waiting in the waiting room, prior to being ushered to the consultation room, I picked up a copy of a magazine that depicted the host from *Who Wants to Be a Millionaire?* on the cover. When Dr. Durrel arrived, I showed him the cover picture of the game show host, Regis Philbin, and said that this is exactly why I am reluctant to have any cosmetic surgery performed. I pointed out how bad the man looks because his upper eyelids have been drawn back so far. He agreed the plastic surgery the man received does look bad but that there are different procedures for men and for women. He showed me that men's eyebrows go straight across and that women's eyebrows, such as my own, are more curved, so the eyelid procedure is different and that whoever did the man obviously did not know the difference. I asked him if he remembered me from the last visit and he said that he did. I said that I was still reluctant, and I mentioned the terrible facelift I see on Barbara Walters. Then, I told him, I just wanted to be honest with him. I said that over the last five years I had visited with several plastic surgeons (all very true) and that I still felt reluctant. I said that each surgeon had recommended something a little different and that I was now even more confused than ever. I said that Dr. Wallace in Miami had recommended a forehead lift but that his partner was passing by the room and when he heard Dr. Wallace's recommendation, he gave him a dirty look. Then, I said I contacted a Dr. David Marks in Santa Monica, California, who had me send him photographs. He recommended no cutting, only liposuction to my face. Then I mentioned that I consulted with Dr. Mack, who wanted to also perform eyelid surgery, Dr. Franklin, who recommended a forehead lift, like Dr. Wallace, and I threw in Dr. Rosen for good measure. I said that I was most impressed with Dr. Franklin and that my final decision was between him and Dr. Franklin, who had impressed me immensely.

At this point, Dr. Durrel went into full-fledged overload on me. He began talking very rapidly and very defensively. I wish I was permitted to tape-record this barrage of words that fell upon me, but I am not. So, let's see. This is all my best from memory. He referred to Dr. Franklin as a "butcher." He said Dr. Franklin was not even a real plastic surgeon, unlike himself who went through seven plus years of special training. He said that Dr. Franklin is so bad that he should not be permitted to be in business. That Dr. Franklin will perform any procedure on anyone, just for the money, that Dr. Franklin is non-selective, that he has testified in court against the man on dozens of cases, that Dr. Franklin has been sued dozens of times, that he used to be a dentist and that he attended some kind of weekend seminar at one time and was given a license to become a plastic surgeon but that he is not board certified and that he got into so much trouble in Miami that he moved to Gainesville to get away from the heat. I think he said that they took away his license in Miami and also that his reputation in Gainesville is so bad that they will not permit him to perform surgery at Florida Hospital. Instead, Dr. Franklin, the butcher, has to send his patients to a small clinic in Hamptonville to perform surgery. He said that Dr. Franklin and people like Dr. Franklin should not be permitted to perform plastic surgery; that he is not a REAL plastic surgeon, but a FAKE one. He then went on to say that people like me are problem people and that actually I could go see anyone I want and that, at this point, he would not even want me to be his patient because he could already tell that I would be unhappy and dissatisfied because I have unrealistic expectations of cosmetic surgery results. Somehow, we got onto the subject of

Michael Jackson. Oh, I remember, it was because he said that trusting patients of his are repeat patients who have a little bit done at a time, and I said, "Sounds like Michael Jackson." And again, he jumped on my case and said, "See. There you go again. Going to an extreme." He said that Michael Jackson represents an extreme and that if Michael Jackson walked into his office right now he would send him out the back door and not do a single procedure to him because he is a plastic surgery freak. He said that because I think of plastic surgery in such extremes he would be very reluctant to work with me but that butchers, such as Dr. Franklin, would take me on, and that is my prerogative. He said that he has done post-surgery plastic surgery on several of Dr. Franklin's botched jobs over the years and has testified against him on several occasions in a court of law.

At that point, the phone in Dr. Durrel's consultation room rang. He told me to sit tight and that he'd be back shortly.

Twenty minutes passed. Actually, at the end of ten minutes, I was ready to leave. I felt I already had obtained a great earful to write a great report, but then I thought, "Let's see just how long he makes me wait." After about twenty minutes, he returned. This time, he had a little more composure. Appearing a little calmer, and apologizing for the wait, he asked me if I had any further questions. I said I didn't. He said he would send me back to Julie and have her show me photos of REAL patients of his, not fake pictures like Dr. Franklin uses. He said that when Dr. Franklin goes to these weekend "Learn to be a plastic surgeon" conferences, they give him fake pictures to put in his waiting room to entice patients into seeing glorious results. "Then, if you're not pleased with the real results, Dr. Franklin just refuses to see you any further," he said.

Julie was busy at the moment, so Dr. Durrel ushered me into another little conference room until Julie got off the phone. At that point, Ramona spoke with me at length. I initiated a conversation, saying, "Wow. It's pretty slow here today." She said, "That's because it's Tuesday. It's also slow here on Tuesday mornings and afternoons because we perform surgery on Tuesday evenings." She added, "Come back here on Wednesdays and Thursdays and you'll see lots of patients." I asked her if it was really true that Dr. Franklin is not a real plastic surgeon and that Dr. Durrel has had to redo a lot of Dr. Franklin's botch jobs. She shook her head emphatically. "Why does that happen?" I inquired. She said that Dr. Franklin performs too many procedures all at once and so the results are sometimes going to be really bad. You can only do a little bit at each cosmetic surgery session. She said that unlike Dr. Franklin, Dr. Durrel has never ever been sued. She said that you can look on the Web and check to see which doctors are being sued. She also mentioned Dr. Rosen having a woman die from liposuction, although when I was speaking with Dr. Durrel, he said that both Drs. Rosen and Mack were okay guys because they had the board certified years of training and were REAL plastic surgeons, just like himself.

It was now time to see Julie again. I told her I no longer had the price paper from August 18, so she gave me another copy of it from my file. We talked a little more about my mom and she reassured me that my mother would be okay. The photos she was supposed to show me of "real" patients were not revealed. She told me there was "no charge" for today's consultation, perhaps because it was only about 10 minutes, and the rest of the time I was left alone in the consultation room.

END OF REPORT

Points to Remember: What made this assignment a success?

1. By naming several plastic surgeons, the surgeon I was investigating did not suspect that his competitor had hired me.
2. By acting ditzy and confused, the surgeon did not suspect that he was under investigation, even though he clearly knew that I am a private investigator.
3. Good listening and memory skills. By listening carefully, I was able to memorize most of the conversation, almost verbatim. One comment I left out, I later reported to my client: He had also referred to his competitor as "incom-

petent." My client decided to sue the other plastic surgeon
and he won.

Seven Years of Jail Time
— Suspended!

I often pray that I'll be working for the good guys when I
do a P.I. job. I say that sincerely. So, it was with some am-
bivalence that I took on the job of trying to get a young man
who had been part of a car theft ring off the hook from jail
time.

First thing I did, as always, was to listen carefully to his
story. After listening to him and diligently transcribing the
tape, I did believe he was guilty. In fact, he admitted that he
was the one who switched out the engines on stolen vehicles.
But was jail the answer? The man had two small children.
He was a first time offender. He promised me that, if acquitted, he would never again become involved in any kind of
illegal activity. I tended to believe him.

This was my first federal court case. The attorney I worked
for took my investigative reports quite seriously. Most of her
defense testimony hinged upon my findings.

Our man was, indeed, acquitted. I was stunned. My investigation actually got the guy out of seven years of jail. His
family came up to me afterwards and hugged me, with tears
in their eyes. I had to turn away and catch the elevator so
they wouldn't see that I was becoming emotional. My investigation had been a success. What I did was discredit the
main witness against our client by finding dirt on him.
Criminal defense can be rewarding, especially when you're
defending someone who has already learned his lesson.

Digging Up Dirt on Ms. Davidson

An out-of-state attorney hired me to investigate a woman who had filed a federal lawsuit against her former employer for sexual harassment and gender discrimination in the workplace. The attorney who represented the company, Ms. Jane Franks, directed me to obtain sworn statements from former and current employees who were familiar with the plaintiff, Ms. Andrea Davidson.

Prior to interviewing the employees, I read the allegations that Ms. Davidson had lodged against the company in her lawsuit. According to Ms. Davidson, who was the former human relations director, she was continually and repeatedly sexually harassed by male employees. There were a couple of e-mails with off color jokes attached to the court papers as evidence. Ms. Davidson also claimed that men were given preferential treatment over women and that they were often promoted over well-qualified women with more seniority.

The attorney provided me by fax with a list of questions that I should ask the interviewees. From this base of questions, I was then supposed to formulate my own questions in order to obtain relevant information.

I interviewed 18 potential witnesses in all. What struck me most were the amazing similarities in their recollections. According to the witnesses, it was Ms. Davidson who was the sexual harasser. She had openly flirted with several of the men in the workplace and had even allegedly engaged in sexual intercourse with two men. She had a reputation for being very foul-mouthed; she spent time at work playing games on her PC; she failed to turn in timely reports; she had to be called in by the supervisor repeatedly for failing to perform her job duties as specified in her job description. She harped and complained constantly and when she discovered, via the daily newspaper, that a large corporation had just been sued by all of its female employees for gender discrimination, she photocopied the newspaper article and placed a copy in each of the female employees' mailboxes. When the manager discovered what she had done, he called her into his office for the umpteenth time and demanded an explanation. Ms. Davidson claimed that **all** of the female employees believed there was gender discrimination in the workplace and that **all** of them were quite disgruntled and dissatisfied with the atmosphere at the company.

The manager is a man who likes to take action immediately when there is a perceived problem. He therefore called an impromptu meeting right on the spot of **all** management and asked them to go ahead and air their complaints against him and/or the company. No one had anything to say. It turned out that if there was any griping going on within the management ranks, it could simply be classified as "catharsis" — venting to let off normal work-related frustration. But no one came forth and supported Ms. Davidson in her company-bashing statements. Shortly thereafter, Ms. Davidson was terminated and she, in turn, filed the federal lawsuit.

After obtaining the sworn statements from the 18 witnesses, I then delved deeper into Ms. Davidson's past. Using her résumé as a starting point, I contacted all of her former employers. The first man I contacted spoke of Ms. Davidson in glowing terms. He said that she had been very personable with his customers and had helped him to take his business from a one-man operation to a full-fledged business. At the end of these praises for Ms. Davidson, I asked him if he would happen to know of any other companies where Ms. Davidson had worked either before or after the time he had employed her. "Yes," he replied. "She also worked for some time for a colleague of mine located right down the street." I jumped back in my car and headed straight away to the next location.

It was raining heavily when I arrived at the establishment of Mr. Mooney, who owns an equipment leasing business. He was in the middle of assisting a customer when I approached him, so I sat and waited for a considerable amount of time. Finally, Mr. Mooney joined me in the waiting room. "Yes, ma'am, how can I help you?"

I introduced myself and provided Mr. Mooney with a business card. "I understand from your competitor down the road that Ms. Andrea Davidson is a former employee of yours?"

Suddenly, the man dropped the friendly smile off of his face. It appeared that every hair on his body was standing. "Yes," he said curtly. "And I'd rather not discuss it. It was the worst year of my life, but that was a decade ago, and I'd just like to put it behind me and never discuss it ever again."

"What happened?" I asked the man.

"I said I won't discuss it," was his reply, and he showed me to the door.

I decided to take a guess. "Would it be that perhaps Ms. Davidson attempted to sue you for workplace discrimination and sexual harassment?" I ventured.

"Yes!" Mr. Mooney replied. "How did you know?"

"Well, Ms. Davidson is now suing **another** company for the same exact charges. I really need your help, Mr. Mooney." I took notice of a poster on his wall indicating that he is a Christian businessman. "Mr. Mooney," I begged, "I believe it is our Christian duty to help our neighbors. Please tell me what happened so we can halt these kind of frivolous lawsuits from repeatedly occurring to others."

Mr. Mooney's face softened. We stood near the exit door and carefully looked into each other's faces. Then suddenly, I realized that I already knew Mr. Mooney from one of my "past lives." "Mr. Mooney!" I declared. "Don't you remember me!?"

"No," he replied.

"You have a daughter named Debra — do you not?"

"That's correct."

"Well, a long time ago, back when Debra was in high school, she was failing algebra. I was her math tutor. I pulled her through that course with flying colors. Do you remember me?"

Mr. Mooney's face brightened. "Oh, yes! Of course!"

Suddenly, Mr. Mooney was willing to disclose all the information regarding Ms. Andrea Davidson. He escorted me into his back office.

Mr. Mooney then explained to me that after six months of employment Ms. Davidson had sued him on three counts: (1) Workman's compensation (claiming that she had injured her leg on a computer desk), (2) Workplace discrimination and sexual harassment, and (3) Unemployment benefits. In the end, Ms. Davidson had lost on all three counts, but Mr. Mooney had spent a year of his time and several thousand dollars in litigation fees. The more he recalled the past, the more upset he became. Finally, he asked me to leave once again, saying that Ms. Davidson is a very vindictive person and that he really does not want to get involved. "Just forget you even came here," he said. "I was going through these old records just a few days ago and I had decided to throw them away. In fact, my wife was going to shred them tomorrow."

Mr. Mooney then walked me back to the front exit door. "Mr. Mooney," I declared, "would you happen to know any other companies for which Ms. Davidson worked?"

"Yes," he replied. "Prior to working for me, Ms. Davidson worked for Three Rivers State College as a bookkeeper; she also sued them for gender discrimination and sexual harassment."

I called the college's legal department the following morning but all they could tell me was that there had been a case that was settled out of court (Ms. Davidson had lost) and that all their records had been destroyed. "Perhaps the state at the capital still has copies of the hearings," the administrative assistant suggested.

Meanwhile, I recontacted Mr. Mooney and attempted to persuade him to let me photocopy at least some of the documents. His records were not on file in any courthouse. This time, Mr. Mooney gave me the name of his attorney. "If it's okay with him, then perhaps I'll cooperate with you," he stated.

For two days, employees in the state capital attempted to find old microfilm records regarding Ms. Davidson's suit against the college. Finally, on the third day, a 19-page document was faxed to me. Reading through this document, I discovered that there was **another** employer — prior to Ms. Davidson working for the college — whom she had also sued for similar allegations.

After a week of investigating every facet of Ms. Davidson's life I discovered the following information:

❑ That she had sued a total five former employers for sexual harassment and workplace discrimination.

❑ That the automobile she drives actually belongs to an older gentleman in another state; she signed a promissory note agreeing to pay the gentleman $10,000 over a period of five years. He had not heard from her in three years and she had never made a single payment.

❑ That there was **another** older gentleman who had promised to transfer the title of his car into her name but he had reneged on his offer. She then contacted the police and claimed he had raped her.

❑ That she had been married three times and that she had taken two of her ex-husbands to court repeatedly alleging that they had physically abused her. I also spoke to the new wife of her first ex-husband who told me they had been through hell with Ms. Davidson and that she was still collecting back child support from them, even though her sons are now in their early thirties.

❑ That she had battled with one of her daughter-in-laws and the woman went to the court seeking an injunction against Ms. Davidson, since she feared for her life.

Two weeks after beginning the investigation, Ms. Franks flew into town to take Ms. Davidson's deposition. The all-day questioning took place in Ms. Davidson's attorney's office and I was present for the hearing. It was fascinating to watch the fruits of my work unfold. First of all, it was strange to face someone whom I had never met and yet I knew every facet of this woman's life. Every question that Ms. Franks asked Ms. Davidson, I could have answered. I therefore knew when she was lying and when she was telling the truth. I kept a checklist on a legal pad and wrote additional questions that Ms. Franks could ask the plaintiff as the day progressed.

In the morning, Ms. Davidson talked about previous jobs she had held. However, the five employers that she had sued were never mentioned.

In the afternoon, Ms. Franks brought forth many obscure documents which I had dredged up — none of which appeared in courthouse records anywhere (including records that Mr. Mooney finally turned over to me after six very diplomatic visits to his business). I would pay a week's salary just to have a videotape of the look on Ms. Davidson's face when Ms. Franks presented her with old documents from her past litigations. She appeared to be having menopausal hot flashes all afternoon and her arms, face, and neck were covered with a heavy film of perspiration.

During the last hour of the questioning, Ms. Franks brought up all the quotes from the 18 witnesses I had interviewed. "Ms. Davidson, do you recall pinching Mr. Palacheck on the butt? Do you recall saying to Lori Knud, 'He's a little on the short side but he'll do?' Do you recall administering oral sex to Jason Lang in the parking lot? Do you recall telling Mr. Mache that 'Any time he's ready, you're ready?' And that he should check out your big breasts — which you referred to as 'pillows?'" These types of questions went on and on for several pages. There must have been more than a hundred questions in all. To which Ms. Davidson replied with shock and horror after each question, "No! I have no recollection of that whatsoever! That's totally not true! It's all fabricated!!" As I sat there, poker-faced, all afternoon, I couldn't help but think that Ms. Davidson had taken a course in denial taught by William Jefferson Clinton.

After Ms. Davidson denied each and every allegation, Ms. Franks eyeballed Ms. Davidson intensely and said, "So, you mean to tell me that (she named all 18 people) are all lying?"

"Yes!" Ms. Davidson declared.

It was now almost 6 p.m. Ms. Franks glanced at her watch, leaned back in her chair and announced, "I think we're just about finished here." Within a few minutes, the court reporter was packing up her equipment and Ms. Davidson and her attorney had left the conference room. The court reporter commented, "Gee, these things are always pretty interesting, but this one was **really** interesting."

Ms. Franks skipped out of the building and asked me, "Where can we go to get a beer?"

At the local Holiday Inn we laughed and toasted our mugs.

"I must tell you something," Ms. Franks said, leaning forward. "I am considered to be one of the top attorneys in the

U.S. During my 20 years of practicing law, I have dealt with many fine private investigators, and I would say that you are one of the **best**."

"Why, thank you very much," I replied.

"No. I take that back," she added. "You are **the best** private investigator I have ever worked with."

Yes, indeed. And I agree.

This case made me quite aware of one thing: Companies would be wise to hire private investigators up front to conduct background checks of any potential employee. If the manager had hired me to do just a one-day search of Ms. Davidson, I would have found out enough during one day that he would not have hired her. This, in turn, would have saved his company thousands of dollars and hundreds of hours of wasted time and emotional trauma. There are many Ms. Davidsons out there these days just waiting to make a legal ruckus out of a workplace. Beware!

Chapter Eight
Skip-Tracing

I always love when an attorney calls me and says that he's attempted to find someone using all of his Internet search programs and has failed, so now, he suddenly wants to pay for my services. For the most part, attorneys will try to do the work of a P.I., but when all else fails, they call upon us to do the dirty work.

In reality, I feel that using pretexts and the telephone can get me far more results on finding missing people than any computer or the Internet. First of all, the information on computers is sometimes very out-of-date or even inaccurate. Second, the types of people who skip out know how to trick computers. They know how to stay out of computer databases and are not inclined to change their driver's license address when they move to a new town. The following are cases in which I found those difficult-to-locate persons.

Where's The Dentist?

A large law firm had spent several hours trying to locate a dentist for one of their prime cases. At the end of several days of searching, they faxed me a copy of their dead-end results and asked me to spend two hours on the case to "see what I could come up with." They, of course, were convinced that if none of their high-powered attorneys or professional legal researchers had not found the guy, a lowly P.I. would certainly not be able to do so, either. However, at the end of two hours, I was closer to finding their man than they had been. So, now they gave me an unlimited number of hours and a phone account to locate him. With much time, diligence, and expense, we got our man. It turned out he was now practicing dentistry in Israel. Here's what I did.

1. **The law firm had traced him from Florida to Brazil.** At that point they stopped, saying that the next step would entail a Portuguese translator. By luck, I happened to have a friend who is studying at the university. A native of Brazil, she worked as an attorney in her country and she is extremely brilliant.

2. **Calling Brazil was costly, but within a few hours, we had obtained information that the dentist in question was registered as a full-time graduate student at the University of São Paulo.**

3. **Checking for research publications, we discovered that the dentist had been one of four researchers who had published an article on TMJ (a clicking of the jaw which indicates the jaw is out of alignment) in 1998.**

4. **Next, we called the publishers of the journal.** The journal had no names and addresses of the four dentists on file, but they did have the phone number and address of a professional organization affiliated with the journal.

5. Checking with the professional organization, we obtained potential addresses for two of the four dentists in Israel.

6. We also checked the address which was listed for a Dr. Leeburg (not our guy) who was the first listed of the four dentists who wrote the article. Using international directory assistance, we obtained two overseas phone numbers for a medical center which he listed as his business address on the publication.

7. Both numbers turned out to be unusable. One was a fax number. We certainly did not want to send a fax. It would be too obvious that we were searching for his partner. The second number was disconnected. Checking back with international directory assistance (at $7.50 per call), I was told that there were no other numbers listed for the medical center in Ashkelon, that it must have gone out of business.

8. Calling back to Brazil, we located the chairman who supposedly is interning the dentist we were trying to find. He said that Dr. Barzon had not been seen for the last six months and it was rumored that he had moved to Israel (although the computer records at the university in São Paulo still indicated he was currently a full time student).

9. Rising at 2:30 a.m., I began calling Israel for the third day in a row. This time, I obtained the number for the Ministry of Health. When they answered the phone, I would say, "Good morning, hello, how are you?" Immediately, everyone I contacted switched over to English and replied, "I am fine. How are you?"

   "Do you have a board of professional regulations which lists the names and addresses for dentists practicing in Israel?"

"Yes, we do. And you have reached it," the voice said.

I told her I needed the names and addresses for four dentists in Israel.

She said, "We just don't blindly pass out this information to anyone. Why do you need it?"

"Because I, too, am doing research on TMJ and I wish to contact the dentists and offer my assistance."

She bought the pretext and spilled forth the names and addresses and phone numbers for all four of the dentists.

Two were located in Ashkelon (at the center I thought was closed), and two were in Jerusalem.

First, I called Jerusalem. I confirmed the addresses and phone numbers of two of the four. Now, I knew, if worse came to worst, I could call them directly and ask them for the names and phone numbers of their other two colleagues.

Next, I tried the new number I had obtained for the medical center in Ashkelon. By this time, it was about 11:30 a.m., Israeli time. I spoke with a young, female receptionist for the medical center.

"Yes!" she replied. "They both work in this building. Would you like their office phone numbers, or would you like their cell phones?"

"How 'bout both?" I said.

She also provided me with their mailing addresses, and their e-mail addresses.

It had taken a total of about eight hours and hundreds of dollars in long distance phone calls, but I got my man. In fact, I got more information than my clients had requested. They were thrilled and impressed with the results.

Points to Remember: What made this assignment a success?

1. **Always try to think in multiple directions when trying to find someone.** The law firm had only looked on the Internet and this had taken them to Brazil. The information they obtained laid a good foundation for me, but it was only a beginning. My thinking in multiple directions led me to:

   - Contact a professional journal
   - Discover there was a professional association connected to the journal
   - Contact the dentist's graduate professor
   - Contact international directory assistance and attempt to contact the primary journal author
   - Contact the Department of Professional Regulations, known as the Ministry of Health, in Israel
   - Contact the two health centers, one in Jerusalem, one in Ashkelon, until I finally got my man.

   If I had thought only in terms of confining my search to Brazil (which is where the attorneys assumed the dentist was located), he would never have been found. By being a poly-directional thinker, I was able to obtain his true whereabouts.

2. **Always have a pretext.** If I had told the woman at the Ministry of Health the true nature of my mission, she certainly would not have provided me with the medical centers where the four dentists are operating.

Finding the Bank Loan Officer

An attorney contacted me and said he had checked the Internet for a former bank loan officer. He had found three persons with such a name on the Internet, but none seemed to be the man he was attempting to locate. Did I have any suggestions?

In ten minutes, I called the attorney back. I had located the home address of his man.

Here's what I did.

1. **I called the bank where the man used to be a loan officer.** Posing as a ditzy customer, I asked the receptionist who answered the phone for his extension.

   "He no longer works here," she said in a flat tone.

   "Oh, my!" I declared. "He told me he would help me get a loan. He is such a nice man! I have dealt with him many times in the past. Did he transfer to another bank?"

   "Not that I know of."

   "Well, do you know what city he might have moved to?"

   "He hasn't moved to any other city. He's still right here. He comes into the bank and banks here all the time."

   "Oh. Well, thank you very much. Please tell him I said 'hi' the next time you see him."

2. **I next called the Property Appraiser's Office.** Sure enough, they had a homestead property and address on file for the man.

   Within ten minutes, I was able to call back the attorney and give him the address.

   "My, you're good!" he said. "You could have waited a couple of hours and billed me more," he said.

   "I know," I told him. "But I'm not that kind of person. I'll pretext like crazy, but I am extremely truthful and above board with my clients."

   That attorney is now a regular client of mine.

Points to Remember: What made this investigation a success?

1. **Pretext.** A ditzy bank customer calls up to inquire about her favorite loan officer. The information she obtains gives enough clues that the man can then easily be found. Keep in mind: the attorney was led to believe that the loan officer had left town when he quit his job. Hence, his futile Internet search. By calling the bank first, I was able to discover that the man was, indeed, still in the same city.

2. **Property addresses are a matter of public record.** I assumed that anyone who holds a position of bank loan officer is wealthy enough to own his own home. My assumption was accurate.

3. **If he had not owned property, I next would have contacted the utilities company and attempted to find a valid address on the man.**

Linoleum or Tile?

A woman contacted me by phone and she sounded very distraught. About a month ago, she and her girl-friend/neighbor had been enjoying happy hour at a local bar when they were approached by two men wearing business suits who asked both of them to dinner. The women had noticed the men sitting with a group of other well-dressed men discussing a law case. The two men took the two women out on separate dates, dined them, and then said they were very interested in them. Both felt that the women were potential marriage partners. The woman who contacted me was particularly impressed with the man who dined her every day for three days. In fact, by the end of the third day, she did something completely out of character. She joined him that evening in his Marriott hotel room and they made love. The next morning, the man said he was boarding a plane with his law firm partners for Puerto Rico. He had said that he was the head of a large San Francisco-based law firm. Together, he and his partners solved international cases, such as the case of an overseas firm that was producing toys using the name "Mattel." He promised to contact her upon his return from Puerto Rico.

The woman, divorced with two children, and a struggling secretary, felt this was a dream come true. A rich man was interested in her.

Three weeks passed. Neither she nor her girlfriend had heard anything from the two men. Disappointed, she had attempted to contact his law firm in San Francisco, but there was no firm either under the name of Roger Marcus (the man who dated her) or Michael West (the man who had dated and slept with her neighbor friend). Would I be able to find the attorneys?

The first thing I did was call the Marriott hotel and see if they would give me any information. None of the pretexts I used seemed to work, so then I called back and simply asked what companies had rented the banquet facilities for meetings on those particular dates. There were three companies — a dental firm, Amway, and Amtico Flooring, based in Trenton, New Jersey. None of these meetings seemed to have any connection with San Francisco. Hence, I called all of them at their various locations and asked the name of their in-house lawyers. None of them had attorneys by either the names of Roger Marcus or Michael West.

I felt I had reached a dead end. I was just about to call the woman back and tell her that it would be impossible to discover a phone number and address for a Mr. Roger Marcus. I even doubted if either one of them had used their real names. I called back the law departments for the dental association and Amtico Flooring and asked if their attorneys had recently attended a meeting at the Mariott in Orlando. The answer was, again, a negative. I sighed and decided I had run out of strategies.

Then I made one last phone call. I called back to Amtico Flooring, but this time, I simply asked the switchboard operator to connect me to Roger Marcus, not the law department. To my surprise and amazement, I next heard a receptionist announce, "Roger Marcus' office. How may I help you?"

"This is the office of Attorney Roger Marcus?"

"This is the office of Roger Marcus," she corrected me, "but he is not an attorney."

"Oh. Well, what is he?" I inquired.

"He is the head of our sales department. He specializes in linoleum and tile."

"Oh, I see. And did he and his sales associates recently attend a meeting in Orlando, Florida?"

"Yes. I believe that is correct."

I was flabbergasted. A group of salesmen posing as high-powered attorneys, probably hiding their wedding bands in their wallets.

I next called the library and had the reference librarian look up Mr. Roger Marcus in her city directory. There he was — name, address, name of his wife (Nancy). They have one child. What a sleaze.

My client should have called him and claimed she was pregnant. I don't think she contacted him ever again. But we were both amazed at what a man would go through just to get a date.

Does Mary Lou Still Work Here?

Mr. Kelly obtained my business name and number from long-distance information. He was calling from Michigan and he needed to find his wife so he could serve her with divorce papers and possibly get back his truck. She had split two months earlier with their five children and her boyfriend, whose child she was carrying. Mr. Kelly wanted me to find out where she works and her home address and phone number. He said she has several relatives in the area but all of them were helping to keep her location a secret.

I began this investigation by asking Mr. Kelly for as much information as possible. He provided me with the make and model of the vehicle, names and addresses of relatives in the area, and some (it turned out) very poor directions. All of Mrs. Kelly's relatives lived in far away places out in the country. Finding them was almost an impossible task.

I brought along my handy door-to-door cosmetic kit and was prepared to give away five-dollar certificates to any relative I located. I knew that with a foot in the door, I could then offer additional certificates if the relative provided me with the name and address of any other relatives I could contact. Hopefully, Mrs. Kelly's name and address would be one of the addresses with which they would provide me.

After several hours of searching, I did manage to find one of Mrs. Kelly's cousins. However, she was in the middle of hosting a backyard barbeque. She was interested in obtaining $5 worth of free cosmetics and told me to come back the next day. However, as it turned out, I never had to return.

That evening, around 9 p.m., after a futile attempt to find Mrs. Kelly all day long, I drove to the local supermarket to pick up and cash the Western Union payment that Mr. Kelly had wired. While the cashier processed the payment, I suddenly heard a voice in my head asking a question, so I decided to act upon that voice. It seemed a little weird to take advice from a voice in my head, but I had nothing to lose.

"So, does Mary Lou Kelly still work here?"

The cashier looked up from the register. "Yeah. She's right over there." Using his thumb, he pointed over his shoulder.

"Well, at least, I thought she was over there," he continued, looking over his shoulder. "She must have gone on break. Do you want me to page her for you?"

It was all I could do to conceal my shock and delight. "Oh, no! We're old friends from Michigan. She is from Michigan, isn't she?"

"Oh, yes. Flint, Michigan. She just moved down here a couple of months ago."

"Yes, of course. We're old high school classmates! Wait until she finds out that I'm down here, too! She will be so surprised! Listen, can you help me surprise her?"

"Sure."

"I'd like to send her some flowers or something to let her know I'm in town. Do you send flowers from this store?"

"No. But there's a flower shop right down the street."

"Great! Can you write down their name and address?"

"No problem."

"Oh! And I'll need her home address and phone number, too."

"Let me go into the office and get that information for you."

When he handed me Mrs. Kelly's address on a little piece of paper, I couldn't rush out of that store fast enough! As soon as I safely entered my car and pulled away, I burst into hysterical laughter.

Mission accomplished!

Points to Remember: What made this investigation a success?

1. **Always have several angles from which you can attempt to locate someone.** In this case, I could have re-contacted her cousin the following day. I also had the address of Mrs. Kelly's mother, and that was another card I could have played.

2. **Trust your hunches.** A woman, new in a small town, unskilled, seeking instant employment. Some obvious places to search (using the same "assumption question" I posed):

   • The supermarket
   • Local restaurants
   • The bank
   • A doctor's office, as receptionist
   • Dry cleaners
   • Gift shop
   • Discount department stores

   You get the idea. I could have contacted a number of these places and asked to speak with her. After that, I could have contacted the local utilities company to have obtained her home address and phone number.

Talking With a 31-Year-Old Child

A mother hired me to go talk to her son, if I could find him. He had been living in a trailer park but had recently been evicted. George promised his mom a few weeks back that he would leave Gainesville and move to Orlando with his uncle. But he still hadn't shown up and his mother from North Carolina worried that he was doing too many drugs and alcohol and would end up dead. Mother and son had not gotten along for a long time. The relationship was extremely strained. Mom wanted to know if I, as a psychologist and as a P.I., would talk to her boy and see if I could convince him to go to Orlando. I said I would give it a try.

I staked out for several hours in front of his trailer, which had an eviction sign posted on the front door. His items remained inside, said the office manager at the trailer park. She was certain that if I waited long enough, he'd show up to get something out of his place, even though the electricity had been cut off.

Around 6 p.m., George did, indeed, show up at his old residence. He walked up to the door, removed the eviction notice, and headed back to his car, the engine still running. I rushed over to him, clad in a sun dress and a large brimmed straw hat.

"George?" I asked in a sweet tone.

"Yes." He was already in his vehicle, engine running and about to pull away.

"Could you hold on a minute? I'd like to talk with you."

"Who are you?"

"George, my name is Angelina and your mother sent me to talk with you."

George's shoulders drooped, but he turned off the engine.

"What now."

"Your mother is greatly concerned about you. She wonders why you haven't gone to your uncle's house in Orlando, as you said you would do."

"I'm on my way tomorrow," he said. "Trust me."

I could smell alcohol on his breath.

"George," I continued. "Your mom wants to make sure you have a plan for your life."

"I do," he said. "I just came from the community college today. I plan to transfer all of my credits and continue my education in Orlando."

"I think that's a great idea. And what about your drinking?"

"I am going to start attending AA meetings when I get to Orlando," he said. He sounded sincere.

"I hope you will keep your word on these promises," I said.

"I will. I'm tired of spinning my wheels," he confessed. "Tell my mother that I'm glad she sent you. Tell her I love her and that I will call her when I get to Orlando."

George did keep his word. A few days later I received a thank you call from George's mom. "Your visit made a big difference. He realized just how much I care. He is keeping all of his promises. I am so grateful."

Is Mony Still in Town?

A mother, Mrs. Higgins, contacted me and wanted to know if her son's ex-girlfriend still resided in Alachua County. Ten years ago, the girlfriend pressed criminal charges against Mrs. Higgins' son. He was found guilty, and part of the settlement was that he agreed to never set foot in Alachua County as long as his ex-girlfriend resided therein. The report that appears below details all the twists and turns this investigation took. At first, it appeared that the young woman had, indeed, left the county. But upon further investigation, more facts were revealed. Read on.

REPORT TO: MRS. HIGGINS
RE: MONY SHELBY DAVIS

Investigation was conducted August 12 from approximately 3 p.m. until 8 p.m. What seemed straightforward and simple turned out to be a complex investigation with positive results: the whereabouts, etc., of Mony Davis were revealed.

In the first hour of the investigation, I checked records with the utility company. Mony Davis is still listed as the alternate for responsibility for the utility bill at 2955 NW 88 Terrace. The person of primary responsibility is Don Shander, who was listed as working for Brightco (they paint automobiles). A "bad dog" was also listed as being at the residence. Two phone numbers were listed: 555-7979 and (877) 555-3489. At this point, I was under the impression that the investigation was concluded, but I double checked by calling 555-7979 and discovered that the number is disconnected. Next, I called Brightco and asked to speak with Don Shander. He has not worked for Brightco for the last two years. I then called (877) 555-3489: this is the number for the Shalimar Theater in Lewistown and they had never heard of Mony Davis.

Next, I generated a lengthy $100 report from DBT, which is included. According to the DBT report, Mony Davis lives at 3329 NE 54th Place. I called back the utilities company and discovered that the utility bill is registered to a man in his nineties at that address. There is also one vehicle at that address — again, it turned up registered to a Mr. Patrick Henrod, who was born 5/12/10. For the next two and a half hours I dialed Mr. Henrod's number. The voice on the answering machine — that of a young woman — said that I had reached 555-5064 or 555-1535 and to leave a message at the tone. I left no messages. When I called 555-1535, the same message played.

I then checked the criss-cross directory and discovered that several other people who were listed as living at 2955 NW 88th Terrace had the last name of Shander — Nick and Tommy. Tommy also previously lived at 4621 NE 82nd Street, and according to DBT records, Mony Davis lived at this same address. It appears that Tommy and Mony then moved in temporarily with Don, Tommy's brother at the 2955 NW 88th Terrace address.

At 7 p.m., with still no answer to the telephone at Mr. Henrod's place, I decided it was time for me to "go sell cosmetics." I am a contracted Beautyco representative. At approximately 7:30 p.m., I arrived at 3329 NE 54th Place. It is an eerie-looking house, painted lime green. The yard is neat. All the lights in the house were turned off. The car that came up in the DBT report was, indeed, sitting in the driveway. There was a newspaper sitting in a plastic bag in the yard.

I next went to the next-door neighbor's house to see if they wanted to buy some cosmetics. In the course of talking to the neighbor man, I asked him when the people next door to him would be home and whether or not I should leave a Beautyco booklet. He said that there was only a very old man living next door and that a female nurse came sometimes to see him. He then said that the old man's daughter lived two doors down on the next street parallel — 53rd Place.

I next went to sell cosmetics at this residence — 3351 NE 53rd Avenue. There were two cars — a red Toyota Celica and a red pick-up truck. A young man, age 17, answered the door. I informed him that his mother had just won $10 worth of cosmetics. His mother, he said, was sick in bed but that he wouldn't mind having the $10 worth of free products. The young man joined me on the front step and together we paged through the latest Beautyco catalogue. He decided he wanted to buy some astringent facial pads — two packages. I informed him that I used to have a friend who lived in the green house on the adjacent street and did he know her — Mony Davis. Oh, yes, he replied. This is his sister. I was speaking with Mony's brother, David Robertswood. David informed me that his grandfather, Patrick Henrod, who resided at 3329 NE 54th Place, had recently died. David and his mother and father planned to move into the green house that Mr. Henrod had resided at. David's mother, Helen, is employed at CYZ Productions.

David informed me that Mony is no longer with Tommy. She has had a new boyfriend for the past year or so whose name is Joseph Shalub. He is from Lebanon, but his entire family has been here in the USA and specifically in town for the past 10 years or so. I told him that I knew Mony back when she was a dancer. "That was a long time ago," he replied. His sister is not working but is supported completely by her boyfriend, whom she plans to marry "soon." They plan to stay in town permanently. For a brief while, she or they lived in Tampa but they enjoy it here and want it to be their permanent residence. Mr. Shalub owns a condo on the tenth floor of the Mead Building. It is apartment either B or C, according to David. Mony Davis' cell phone number is 888-9304. Mony's mom's cell phone number is 888-3884. The mom's name is Helen Robertswood. Helen and David's home phone number is 555-5368.

END OF REPORT

Points to Remember: What made this investigation a success?

1. **Never assume that a disconnected number means that a person no longer resides in a certain town.** Always continue the investigation until you actually speak with the subject or with someone who knows the subject very well.

2. **Do not confine the investigation to the phone.** By going in person to the neighborhood, I was able to thoroughly solve this case.

Chapter Nine
Pretexting

At the Funeral

A man had a reputation for coming on to rich older women and getting them to spend thousands of dollars on him. I was hired to attend a funeral where several people who had taken dance lessons from him would be. Talking with them, I was supposed to find out where he might currently be.

I posed as one of his former dance students. I dressed in black, and when I got to the funeral, I went up to the coffin and thought of everything sad I had ever experienced in my entire life. Soon, I was weeping along with the other mourners.

There was a separate room where they were serving refreshments. After mourning a sufficient amount of time, I entered the hors d'oeuvre room and sat at a long table with several other guests. Soon, I was drawn into the conversation. I talked about my fond memories of John, the dance instructor, who had taught me the fox trot, the waltz, and the tango. But where was he now? Had anyone seen him lately?

One person said that a very good friend of his was sitting at the next table. She would certainly know.

Moving to the next table, I took a chance and said I was friends with the people I had just been sitting with at the other table. Where was John and what was he doing? The woman knew exactly where he was. He was currently on a cruise ship headed to the Bahamas with an older woman he had met while giving dance instructions. She knew the name of the cruise ship, the date it departed, and when it would return. Now, another P.I. could follow him. John, the dance instructor, was known to manipulate funds from his lovers. Now he could be videotaped at the bank and, hence, charges could be pressed against him.

To Find Hidden Assets

An attorney wanted to know if it was worth suing a sleazebag who had ripped off a woman. The attorney said that the sleazebag in question runs a mortgage company, that he makes people pay up front hundreds of dollars to see if they qualify for the loan, and then 99% of the time, he tells them they don't qualify and he keeps their large deposit.

I went to his office to see if I could discover what kind of assets the man possesses. First, there was a brand new Mercedes in the parking garage. Checking with the auto dealership, whose name appeared on the license plate frame, they told me that the car had just been purchased and Mr. Sleazebag owed several thousands.

Next, I went into his office and posed as a person in need of one of his loans. Lucky for me, he stepped out of his office at the very beginning of our discussion before I had to explain too much. While he was gone, I discovered a bank deposit slip on the corner of his desk. I quickly memorized the account number. After departing from his office, claiming I was in a hurry and would come back another day, I called the bank and posed as his wife. I demanded to know the balance. To my surprise, the clerk gave me the balance, which was a negative seventeen dollars. There was one other bank account, but it had been empty for quite some time.

I reported my findings back to the attorney. She decided it was not worth it to try to sue the sleazebag.

Points to Remember: What made this investigation a success?

1. **The attorney had already checked the man's home address.** He was renting an apartment in a run down neighborhood. A check inside his apartment had produced few goods of any value.

2. **Memory power was a key ingredient in this investigation.** By memorizing the man's bank number, I was then able to call the bank and discover the negative funds.

3. **Luck.** Most of the time, I factor luck into my investigations. In this case, I was doubly lucky. Not only did the bank clerk buy my pretext, but the sleazebag had left his office long enough for me to memorize his bank account number.

4. **There would have been another way for me to get his bank account number.** I simply could have paid him a small deposit for a mortgage loan. When the canceled check was returned to me, his bank number would have been written on the back.

To Find Where the Vietnamese
Ex-Girlfriend Works

A woman claiming to be a social worker told me she had been given a budget by her employer to discover if a Vietnamese woman who was applying for free hospital services was, in fact, working. It seemed a little strange to me that a government agency was going out of their way to nab this one individual, but I played along.

For this investigation, I spent several days on the phone making long distance phone calls. All of my calling led to dead ends. I traced the woman to a trailer park where she had once lived. The office told me they remembered that she had resided there with her boyfriend and had not worked. Each time I came across a dead end, the "social worker" paid me hundreds more to continue my investigation.

Finally, there was a break-through. I simply looked up the woman's name in the white pages of the phone book! There she was listed! I called her home and a male with an Oriental accent told me she was not at home, but at work. He instantly provided me with her work number, no questions asked.

I called the work number and it turned out that I just happened to have a friend who works for this same agency. Hence, I was able to find out her department, her supervisor's name, her rate of pay, and how long she had worked for the agency.

But my investigation was not over. I now desired to investigate my client prior to turning over the information. After all, she may have wanted to do physical harm to the woman. After contacting the hospital, I was told by the supervisor of social work that there was no budget for hiring private investigators.

I called back my client and told her I had the name and address of the company, salary, etc. for the Vietnamese woman but I would not release the information to her unless she gave me an honest reason for wanting to know this information. It turned out that the Vietnamese woman was the current girlfriend of my client's ex-boyfriend. Wanting to get even with him, she thought she would turn in the woman who was applying for indigent medical aid to the social service department of the hospital. In so doing, there was no limit to the amount of money she was willing to spend. Altogether, she had spent nearly $1,000 just to get even with her ex-boyfriend by making his girlfriend ineligible for medical assistance.

To Find the Stalker

A college professor contacted me by phone and wanted me to meet with him and his fiancée at the Holiday Inn for supper.

As we sat there enjoying items from the evening buffet, the professor and his girlfriend, Heidi, explained that someone had broken into Heidi's apartment. Although they had filed a police report at the time of the incident, Mr. Professor was willing to spend extra money to help solve this crime. My first questions were: (1) Did the police dust for finger prints? (Yes). (2) What did the thief take?

The answer to my second question was quite surprising. I was expecting to hear that the robber made off with fine jewelry, televisions, computers, and cash. Instead, I was told that the thief took only a handful of items:

- Large jars of peanut butter
- Several cans of tuna fish
- Soiled underwear of Heidi's

- Pictures of Heidi from a body building contest
- One of her favorite gym workout outfits

Now, I don't think it would take Sherlock Holmes to figure out that the suspect in this case was really more of a stalker than a thief. It was obvious that someone was mesmerized with Ms. Heidi. Looking at her, I could understand their fascination. Late twenties, with long blonde hair and a totally muscular body, blue eyes, she appeared to be a human Barbie doll.

My strategy was to go to the gym, work out, and observe the people who watch or interact with Heidi. Her fiancée paid me for one week of workout observation time. By the end of the week, working in conjunction with the local police department, the crime had been solved. Here's what I did: every time I noticed someone interacting with Heidi, I got their fingerprints. For example, there was an Afro-American man who seemed particularly enthralled with Heidi. During his nightly visits to the gym — always timed to arrive and depart in sync with when Heidi arrived and departed — he seemed to spend more time watching her and attempting to interact with her than working out.

On the third night of observation, I bought a 16 oz. bottle of water from the front desk. Approaching him, I told him that I was a new member and asked him if he had any tips on how I could get in shape quickly. As he advised me, I feigned pain in my right foot, then I bent down, untied my shoe, and took out an imaginary stone. While doing this, I had him hold my water bottle. The bottle was then delivered by I.J., who was waiting in the parking lot, to the local police department to determine if there was a fingerprint match. Indeed, there was.

Altogether, I used this same technique on about nine different fellows during the course of that week. But the man I first suspected was indeed the one on whom we obtained a positive fingerprint match. The crime was solved.

In Undercover Drug Investigations

Several apartment complexes allow police officers to have free rent in exchange for simply keeping an eye out on the premises. This fact gave me an idea. If officers could obtain a free apartment, why not a private eye? I called several apartment complexes and suggested free rent in exchange for undercover investigations. I was not surprised when one apartment complex, known as a haven for drug dealers, took me up on my offer. With this apartment, I have the freedom of having an entire work area for my business. In fact, this manuscript was composed from my secret apartment location. Here's what I do:

Every week, I compose a two-page report that I turn into the office manager. Based upon the information contained in these reports, the manager has been able to find reasons to evict drug dealers and also work in conjunction with the local sheriff's department. In my weekly reports, I list names, personal information that tenants have given me, license tag numbers, and the comings and goings of certain vehicles. During the past three months, I have been successful in discovering who are the main players, who are the main buyers, who lives on the premises, and who delivers to the premises. How have I done this?

1. **Direct observation.** I sit on my back porch and simply observe.

2. **Rollerblading.** I roller blade through the apartment complex and take notes with my handy little tape recorder.

3. **Cosmetic sales.** A lot of information has been obtained by interacting directly with the welfare moms who enjoy purchasing my products.

4. **Recently, I hired a pretty, young woman as an intern who poses as my daughter.** She has "befriended" some of the main players and obtained more information as a peer than I possibly could have obtained.

In these weekly reports, I also include all the gossip of the complex. I discovered that the manager really enjoys reading these details, whether it helps her to bust drug dealers or not. I have told her the personal backgrounds of some of her tenants, their habits, fights with their boyfriends, childhood traumas. Some of these reports read more like a Jerry Springer transcript than a private eye report. But that's what keeps her happy. One report simply described all the negative things the welfare moms say about the office manager behind her back.

If you need a free apartment where you can spread out your paperwork and work in privacy, you might want to consider contacting some apartment complexes and making a similar kind of arrangement, as I did. Here's a sample report:

Weekly Report to: Apartment Complex Manager

I now have the name of the third person who hangs out with Mike and Bo. His name is Kelsey, but he goes by his nickname, K. He lives with his mother in building P. The conversation I overheard in the parking lot went like this:

MIKE: K, are you going to be straight by Wednesday?

K: Yeah, I'm going to have my money straight.

MIKE: We should be able to get half.

K: The H.P.? (Note: HP means "half pound" of marijuana)

MIKE: Yeah. If I talk to my boy, we might be able to get the whole thing for five. (i.e., $500 for a pound of weed — which is a really low price, which indicates they are probably selling a lot to get a price that low).

Mike went to his dad's trailer in Oakville, picked up two bags of clothes, and went back to stay in apartment L-l2.

SECOND CONVERSATION:

Bo, Mike, and K attended a church on SW 11th Street with Shyanna, which depicted what happens to sinners, if they don't choose Jesus. One of the characters was a drug dealer. Both Red and K claimed that they could have done a better job playing that part.

Bo, Mike, and K would like to attend church again in the future with Shyanna. The play appeared to make them reflect upon their own lives.

END OF REPORT

"What is My Daughter Doing?"

An out-of-state father, Mr. Tom Bartram, distressed that his 13-year-old daughter, Chastity, had been arrested for shoplifting and thrown out of school for fighting and dressing inappropriately, hired me to discover the details of his daughter's life. He also wanted to know what her mother, to whom he had never been married, was doing. Mr. Bartram and Chastity's mom had lived together for two years in Colorado. "Then she became pregnant and I became 'the asshole," Tom said. "Now she keeps taking me back to court for more and more child support. My daughter just came to visit me for two weeks for the first time in ten years. She was wearing a very revealing top and has her hair dyed. And she's only 13. I'd like to obtain full custody of my daughter and straighten her out before it's too late. I believe her mother is negligent," he told me.

Laying the foundation

This job began with surveillance of the mother's home. However, surveillance turned out to be quite difficult. The mother, Jubie, lives on a dead end dirt road (176th Street) with lots of barking dogs in the neighborhood. Her own yard contained three barking dogs who chased us whenever we drove up and down the street. After three trips to and from the house, we felt concerned that we may have already become too transparent. I had to come up with a plan for getting in and out of the street without raising suspicions. Here are my notes from the first day's report.

Sunday, April 30, 2000
Day I. Preliminary investigation.
Arrived in Alachua with intern investigator, Mr. D.H., in two separate vehicles. Video footage marked "April 30" first shows D.H.s activities; then primary investigator's, Dr. Woodhull. Surveillance showed the following incidents:
9:45 a.m. — arrived on scene. Jubie's car in front of residence.
10:54 — on location. No change in activity.
11:10 — Jubie leaves her residence. Chastity is not with her mom in vehicle. We follow her vehicle. She drives south on 441 and stops at a bank teller machine then goes next door to the convenience store where she purchases a Slurpee (11:23 a.m.). She then heads south again on 441.
11:30 a.m.— I dial from a payphone the home telephone number twice. The first time, the phone rings 14 times; the second time, the phone rings 6 times. No answer. We conclude that Chastity is not at home nor with her mother, which indicates that she slept away from home on Saturday night.
12:08 p.m. — Jubie is seen returning back home. Chastity is not with her.
12:46 p.m. — I drive by the residence, first east, and then west. As I am driving west past the residence I notice that a young

woman has arrived with a young man in a silver car. Jubie is also outside in the front yard.

At this point, we assumed that the young lady was Chastity, with a boyfriend. We ran the tag number on the silver car and found out it was registered to a 19-year-old boy, Matt Ferguson.

For the next several days, as we drove up and down the dirt road, the pattern remained the same: Jubie's green car would be present in the daytime; in the afternoon, Jubie would leave and the silver car would arrive. I gained access to the street without raising suspicions by having two magnetic signs made up which I placed on the front doors of my van — "Ranger U-Pick Farms." These signs were a perfect cover because there just happened to be a real U-Pick farm (with a different name, of course) at the end of the road. Everyone assumed, as I drove up and down the road, that I must be doing business with the local U-Pick Farm.

Using this pretext, I was able to interview several of the neighbors.

Here are more notes from the actual report:

Day 5: Thursday, May 4, 2000
Went to Alachua County Tag office and ran tag of silver car. Car is registered to Matt Ferguson, 19 years old.
10:00 a.m.— Jubie's car at home.

Investigator Woodhull spent day meeting various people in the neighborhood in order to obtain information. Met Frank Parkinson, owner of Parkinson's U-Pick Farm. Mr. Parkinson grows peaches and works as an auditor for the state of Florida. He is 51.

Day 6: Friday, May 5, 2000
Went to Alachua Police Department at 8 a.m. and spoke with the Chief of Police about the 19 year old's car which is frequently seen at Jubie's and Chastity's residence. Three reports came up regarding Matt Ferguson. (1) He was involved in a brawl at Arizona Joe's (a restaurant that is no longer open); (2) He was a suspect in a home burglary; (3) Speeding ticket within the last three months. Address listed at the tag bureau was only a P.O. box. Police did not do much better. They found an address for him on 144th Avenue — a street that runs about 10 miles.

I then spoke with the postmaster, Ben, and yes, indeed, he knows Matt Ferguson and his family. Ben informed me that Matt broke into Ben's home and stole some things and he also broke into another person's home, but neither one of them called the cops because they didn't want to get Matt in trouble with the law. Matt used to associate with Ben's son, who was in major trouble with the law and arrested for selling drugs. Since being reformed, however, Ben's son no longer hangs out with Matt. Ben did give me the exact address on 144th Avenue where Matt's parents live. At 4:30 p.m., we checked their residence. Matt's silver car was parked out front.

Around 8:30 p.m. on Friday evening, as I was about to exit the neighborhood, I noticed that the gate was open, the green car was gone, and the silver car was in the yard at Jubie's residence. It seemed like an opportune time to discover what was going on with a 19-year-old boy and a 13-year-old girl. And so, my "car over-heated" right dead smack in the middle of Jubie's yard. My two other investigators were also conducting surveillance on 176th Street during this entire time period.

I honked my horn and a boy came out of the house, not looking happy to see me in his yard. I introduced myself as Angelina and asked him if he had a cordless phone I could use. He returned shortly with the phone in hand. I then called AAA and told them my car had overheated. They said they'd arrive in about one and one-half hours. Meanwhile, I invited myself inside the house.

The young man, Damon, did not look pleased, but he did not resist either. Once inside the home, I met Matt Ferguson. Both boys were obviously very high on marijuana, judging from their appearance and the aroma inside the home. Matt remained inside Damon's bedroom a good majority of the time I was there, playing violent video games (sounds of explosions) while Damon and I conversed. Twice, Matt left the premises. The telephone rang on several occasions and Matt was always the one to speak with the callers. The conversations were very brief. "I got the stuff. I'll see you in about half an hour." Matt placed one call to his girlfriend, Vicky, whom he resides with in High Springs. Matt wanted Vicky to join him and Damon at Jubie's house when she got off from work, but she was not interested. Matt ended the conversation with the words, "I love you." Matt is a very attractive boy, tall, slender with long blonde hair in wispy curls and perfect features, blue eyes. When I asked him what he does for a living, he said he was currently unemployed.

Description of the Inside of the House
There is a fenced yard, four dogs outside in the yard. There is a screened-in wooden floor porch. I saw three cats — one mother with two baby kittens. The front door leads directly to the kitchen. There were a few dirty cups and dishes in the kitchen but nothing too bad. There was a wooden wreath on the kitchen wall. Damon said his mother made it, that she enjoys crafts as a hobby. Two baskets for the cats were under the kitchen table. The bedroom at the east end of the home belongs to Damon. To the west of the kitchen is Jubie's bedroom, which also doubles as a living room. There is an L-shaped couch on the east and south walls. On the west wall is Jubie's bed. On the long side of the bed is an L-shaped desk, one side is on the north wall. There are two pictures of Jubie's parents — their wedding picture and also a picture of them as old people, on the north side of the desk. There are several papers and books all over this desk. There was also a message scribbled to Damon that told him to water the plants, cut the grass, and feed the dogs over the weekend. Damon indicated that his mother was away for the entire weekend with friends but that is all he would say. Where she was specifically and what she was doing he would not reveal. He also indicated that his little sister was also away for the entire weekend. So, Damon, 18 years old, was given the full run of the house for the entire weekend. Incoming phone calls for Damon and Matt indicated that a party would be ensuing later that evening. There were three envelopes with new photographs in them sitting on top of the desk, but Damon would not share their contents with me.

As we waited the long hour and a half for AAA to arrive, I passed the time by singing songs to Damon and asking him about his taste in music. He was quiet and borderline "paranoid," although Matt was much more jovial and more willing to converse a bit. Matt said that Damon was always pretty shy. Damon did reveal that he works at TCBY and also attends classes at the community college. He is majoring in history but he is going to transfer to a different major, but he's not quite sure what it will be.

Damon said that his mom works from home as a medical transcriptionist.

Damon described his sister, Chastity, as an "annoying" 13-year-old. When asked what makes her so annoying, Damon said that she comes into his bedroom unannounced, uninvited all the time, plops herself on his bed, goes through his stuff, and plays his video games then asks for his assistance in figuring out how to play the games, which he does not wish to give. "I figured out how to play them on my own; you should do the same." Chastity has other 13-year-old girlfriends that she spends the weekends with; she has no boyfriend, according to Damon. Damon said there was a church wedding that his sister, Chastity, would most likely, be attending on Saturday, but that he would not be there.

The far back room on the west side of the home is Chastity's bedroom. I was unable to see this room.

When asked about the neighborhood, Damon said that everyone is okay except for the people next door. When asked what's wrong with them, he said that "They're crazy." I humorously suggested that they might feel the same way about him and his family. He agreed.

Day 7: I had a medical doctor friend of mine call Jubie's home to see if he could get Damon to tell him where his mother might be for the weekend. My friend was going to claim that he needs emergency transcription services. To our surprise, Jubie answered the phone (she was supposed to be out of town for the entire weekend). Jubie said that she is not available for transcription services to an individual doctor because she is under contract with a medical transcription service company.

At 12 noon, I attended the church wedding in an attempt to locate Chastity but I was unable to find her.

Day 8: Obtained records from the Alachua Police Department and also Alachua County Sheriff's Department regarding Jubie and also Damon's friend, Matt Ferguson. I also checked Jubie's residence. She was home until 3:30 p.m. At that time, she left in her car and returned alone at 4 p.m. and again retreated into her home.

On this day, I spoke with Jubie's neighbors, Michael and Greta Mott. I pulled into the Mott's driveway, clad in blue jeans and a white shirt, with my "Ranger U-Pick Farms" sign on my white van. Mr. Mott invited me inside when I handed him a gift basket of peaches that I purchased from the U-Pick farm at the end of the road.

The Motts did not have much time to talk with me, but they were friendly. Mrs. Mott's mother died yesterday and they were on their way to the funeral home. The wake is Wednesday. The death was very unexpected. Her mother was 74.

Mr. Mott said there has been much disturbance and chaos with his neighbor, Jubie, but he did not want to go into too much detail for fear that I may be one of her snooping friends. However, the Motts did inform me that the disputes have involved Jubie's dogs, which run loose on the dirt road, and also a dispute over the well water they share. The Motts and Jubie share a well with six other neighbors. Living side by side, all of them have the same landlady. THE MOTTS HAVE NOT SEEN CHASTITY FOR A LONG TIME, FOR AT LEAST TWO MONTHS, although they did say that Jubie and Chastity do stay inside a lot, so perhaps she is there, but this is what I and my two intern investigators also concluded. We have never seen Chastity during the two weekends or during the week of this investigation. The Motts said that Jubie's son is not a nice person, that he is involved in illegal activity, but they would not specify anything specific. The Motts have two daughters about Chastity's age who used to play with Chastity, but after all the fights, they stopped playing with her. The two girls told me they don't like Chastity anyway.

During the disputes with Jubie, Jubie would hang clothes and garbage on lines right at their joint property line, just to annoy them. And so, the Motts erected a tall, wooden fence in retaliation. The disputes have pretty much ceased since the fence was built.

While seven of the landlady's homes are still on well water and share the same line, the landlady took Jubie off of the well water and put her on city water as part of a way to end the dispute.

END OF REPORT

_____

Chapter Ten
Summary

In this book, we examined case studies and some of the tools used by P.I.s to solve everything from skip-tracing to investigating undercover narcotics, to following and observing cheating spouses. Through these examples, you also learned how to write a report, how to use pretexts, and how to conduct surveillance on a difficult subject. In summary, I'd like to suggest that you always try to keep a fresh perspective when taking on a new case. Never allow yourself to become so busy that you cannot enjoy each case as it is assigned to you. By concentrating thoroughly on each investigation as though it is the sole purpose of your life at that moment, you will, most likely, obtain great results, keep your customers happy, and, of course, continue to enjoy what you are doing.

YOU WILL ALSO
WANT TO READ:

☐ **61145 HOW TO FIND MISSING PERSONS, A Handbook for Investigators, Second Edition,** *by Ronald Eriksen.* This book is the bible for bounty hunters, private investigators, skip-tracers, process servers, repo men, and many others. The author is a no-bull investigator who shows you how to follow someone's trail and how to coax information out of people who would rather not tell. This all-purpose guide is highlighted with case histories from real-life missing persons investigations. If you're looking for someone special, you couldn't ask for a better guide. *1994, 5½ x 8½, 150 pp, illustrated, soft cover.* **$16.95.**

☐ **55117 BE YOUR OWN DICK, Private Investigating Made Easy, Second Edition,** *by John Q. Newman.* Most detective work involves simple research you can do for yourself — if you know where to look. This edition includes information on using the Internet, software, and computer databases, how to find everything about your target's finances, health, employment, pastimes, and "past lives." If you want to know whether someone is rich or a deadbeat, whether they're on the level or a fraud, whether they're cheating on you, stealing from you, or lying to you, then *Be Your Own Dick! 1999, 5½ x 8½, 156 pp, illustrated, soft cover.* **$14.00.**

YOU WILL ALSO
WANT TO READ:

☐ **58075 SATELLITE SURVEILLANCE,** *by Harold Hough.* Once the exclusive tool of governments, satellite technology is now available to anyone. Using actual satellite photos, this book shows you where to buy satellite images, how to enhance and interpret them, and how to hide from "the eye in the sky." Commercial uses include: land and water navigation; pest control; zoning and land-use planning; fighting forest fires; mapping; environmental monitoring; oil and gold exploration; and organizing disaster relief. This book is an essential reference for anyone concerned with the uses and abuses of satellite technology. *1991, 5½ x 8½, 192 pp, illustrated, full color photos, soft cover.* **$21.95.**

☐ **55071 SEX CRIMES INVESTIGATION, A Practical Manual,** *by Burt Rapp.* All sorts of sex crimes are in the news these days — more than ever before. This book is a police manual for the investigation of sex crimes. A practical guide to investigating rapes, prostitution, pornography, child molestation, snuff films, sex in the mail, computer sex crimes, a section on rape prevention, how to develop and exploit information sources, and a complete glossary of terms useful in sex crimes investigations and much more. No modern police or investigative library is complete without this book. *1988, 5½ x 8½, 198 pp, soft cover.* **$16.95.**

YOU WILL ALSO WANT TO READ:

❑ **55052 SHADOWING AND SURVEILLANCE, A Complete Guidebook,** *by Burt Rapp.* Want to tail somebody without them knowing, or conduct a stake-out? This is a no-nonsense guide to shadowing and surveillance techniques with an emphasis on do-it-yourself, low-support methods: Tailing on foot and in a car; how to lose a tail; using decoys and disguises; searching property; photographic surveillance techniques; how to conduct a stake-out; electronic surveillance; and much more. Professional surveillance operatives, police officers, and the private citizen alike can learn from this excellent manual. If you want to keep tabs on an unfaithful spouse, a dishonest employee, or a business competitor, the information you need is right here. *1986, 5½ x 8½, 136 pp, illustrated, soft cover.* **$16.95.**

❑ **40075 SNITCH, A Handbook for Informers,** *by Jack Luger.* Many government and private organizations pay quick cash for the right information. This book will tell you how to gather and sell valuable information. You will learn how to snitch and collect completely anonymously. You will learn how crooks negotiate their way out of prison sentences, how cops treat informers and how to keep from being finked-out yourself. If you are look-ing for an unconventional way to make money, get *Snitch: A Handbook for Informers.* The dirt you dig up could be paydirt. *1991, 5½ x 8½, 145 pp, glossary, index, soft cover.* **$16.95.**

YOU WILL ALSO WANT TO READ:

☐ **19197 STREET SMARTS FOR THE NEW MILLENNIUM,** *by Jack Luger.* Life can be risky for the average citizen. There are criminal elements in our society, as well as pitfalls in our everyday life, which pose real dangers to the safety and security of ourselves and our families. In this unique book, author Jack Luger has provided the methods and resources that enable the reader to minimize these threats to our lives, liberties, and pursuit of happiness. You'll learn to: depend on personal resources instead of police; protect yourself, your family and your assets; and earn untraceable income. So don't be a victim! Learn to be self reliant, and arm yourself with the knowledge that it takes to develop your street smarts and survive this dangerous decade! *1996, 5½ x 8½, 138 pp, soft cover.* **$15.00.**

☐ **58111 THEY'RE WATCHING YOU, The Age of Surveillance,** *by Tony Lesce.* We live in an increasingly transparent world, where practically all of our movements and activities are monitored, and this sometimes frightening book reveals the technology and prevailing philosophy that makes this possible. What the indifferent observers know about you can be hurtful, so it's in your best interest to inform yourself of the extent of the incessant surveillance that is in place, and act accordingly. Contains sections on: surveillance in public; surveillance as intimidation; digging up dirt; surveillance for profit; tools and techniques; and the Internet as a tool. *1998, 5½ x 8½, 136 pp, illustrated, soft cover.* **$12.95.**

YOU WILL ALSO
WANT TO READ:

☐ **55046 LIP READING MADE EASY,** *by Edward B. Nitchie.* Here's a James Bond-type skill every snoop should be familiar with — "listen in" on conversations you can't hear! Find out what deals are being made over seemingly casual lunches. Eavesdrop to your heart's content. Videotape now, translate later. Learn secrets — secretly! Now you can say "I heard it first," even before you hear it. The author taught thousands of people to read lips. His easy-to-use, step-by-step, illustrated method enables you to become a creative spy in just a few short lessons. *1902, 5½ x 8½, 136 pp, illustrated, soft cover.* **$10.00.**

☐ **55082 A PRACTICAL GUIDE TO PHOTOGRAPHIC INTELLIGENCE,** *by Harold Hough.* A guide to taking and interpreting surveillance photographs. Learn how to: take useful photos of objects miles away, and determine their dimensions; read documents burned to an ash; take aerial photographs; use infrared light to capture invisible images; legally use surveillance photographs for commercial purposes, and much more. It doesn't take fancy equipment or extensive training to be a decent surveillance photographer. *1990, 5½ x 8½, 136 pp, illustrated, soft cover.* **$16.95.**

YOU WILL ALSO WANT TO READ:

☐ **58084 DIRTY TRICKS COPS USE And Why They Use Them,** *by Bart Rommel. They make Dirty Harry look like Mr. Clean.* If you think Rodney King had it rough, you ain't seen nothin' yet! Learn how vigilante cops plant evidence, ignore search and seizure laws, conduct illegal interrogations, torture and even execute people. This book details how cops use mace, stun guns, weasel out of Miranda warnings, illegal wiretaps, and other sneaky moves. The law is stacked in favor of creeps, these cops say, and they're out to even the score. If you want to know how the "justice" system really works, get this shocking book! *1993, 5½ x 8½, 160 pp, soft cover.* **$14.95.**

☐ **55083 ESPIONAGE: DOWN AND DIRTY,** *by Tony Lesce.* In the murky world of the spy, hardly anything is as it seems. There are secrets, false identities, cover stories, lies, evasions, denials, and a nerve-racking atmosphere of conspiracy. For some people, this world is attractive. It is also dangerous. What's spying *really* like? Read this book and find out. Covers recruiting, training, infiltration, payment, evacuation, what happens when a spy is exposed, and more. You'll read about how spies are recruited, trained and deployed. How are they paid? What's sex got to do with it? What happens when they are discovered? It's all here. *1991, 5½ x 8½, 174 pp, soft cover.* **$17.95.**

Please send me the books I have checked below:

- ❑ **61145 How to Find Missing Persons, $16.95**
- ❑ **55117 Be Your Own Dick, $14.00**
- ❑ **58075 Satellite Surveillance, $21.95**
- ❑ **55071 Sex Crimes Investigations, $16.95**
- ❑ **55052 Shadowing and Surveillance, $16.95**
- ❑ **40075 Snitch!, $16.95**
- ❑ **19197 Street Smarts for the Millennium, $15.00**
- ❑ **58111 They're Watching You!, $12.95**
- ❑ **55046 Lip Reading Made Easy, $10.00**
- ❑ **55082 A Practical Guide to Photographic Intelligence, $16.95**
- ❑ **58084 Dirty Tricks Cops Use, $14.95**
- ❑ **55083 Espionage Down and Dirty, $17.95**

*We offer the very finest in controversial and unusual books? — A complete catalog is sent **FREE** with every book order. If you would like to order the catalog separately, please see our ad on the last page of this book.*

PIST

LOOMPANICS UNLIMITED
PO BOX 1197
PORT TOWNSEND, WA 98368

Please send me the books I have checked above. I am enclosing $ _____ which includes $5.95 for shipping and handling of orders up to $25.00. Add $1.00 for each additional $25.00 ordered *Washington residents please include 8.2% for sales tax.*

NAME _____

ADDRESS _____

CITY/STATE/ZIP _____

We accept Visa, Discover, and MasterCard. To place a credit card order *only,* call 1-800-380-2230, 24 hours a day, 7 days a week.
Check out our Web site: www.loompanics.com